CUBA

A HISTORY IN ART

Revised edition

Gary R. Libby

With essay and notes by Juan A. Martínez

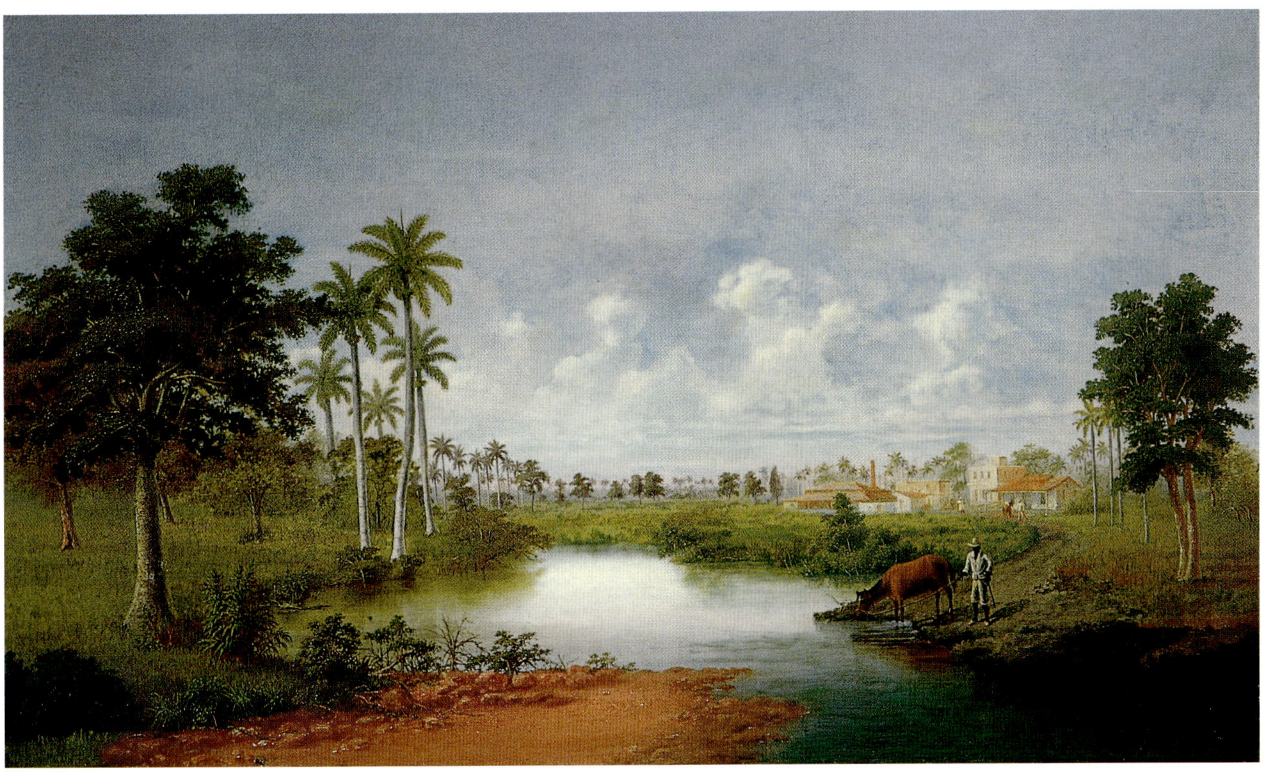

University Press of Florida

Gainesville/Tallahassee/Tampa/Boca Raton

Pensacola/Orlando/Miami/Jacksonville/Ft. Myers/Sarasota

Originally published by the Museum of Arts and Sciences, Daytona Beach 1997
Revised edition 2015

Printed in China on acid-free paper

20 19 18 17 16 15 6 5 4 3 2 1

Author and editor: Gary R. Libby
Assistant editor and author: Juan A. Martínez
Book design: Stacey G. Sather
Photography: James Quine

Library of Congress Control Number: 2014952579
ISBN 978-0-8130-4998-4

The University Press of Florida is the scholarly publishing agency for the State University System of Florida, comprising Florida A&M University, Florida Atlantic University, Florida Gulf Coast University, Florida International University, Florida State University, New College of Florida, University of Central Florida, University of Florida, University of North Florida, University of South Florida, and University of West Florida.

University Press of Florida
15 Northwest 15th Street
Gainesville, FL 32611-2079
http://www.upf.com

Contents

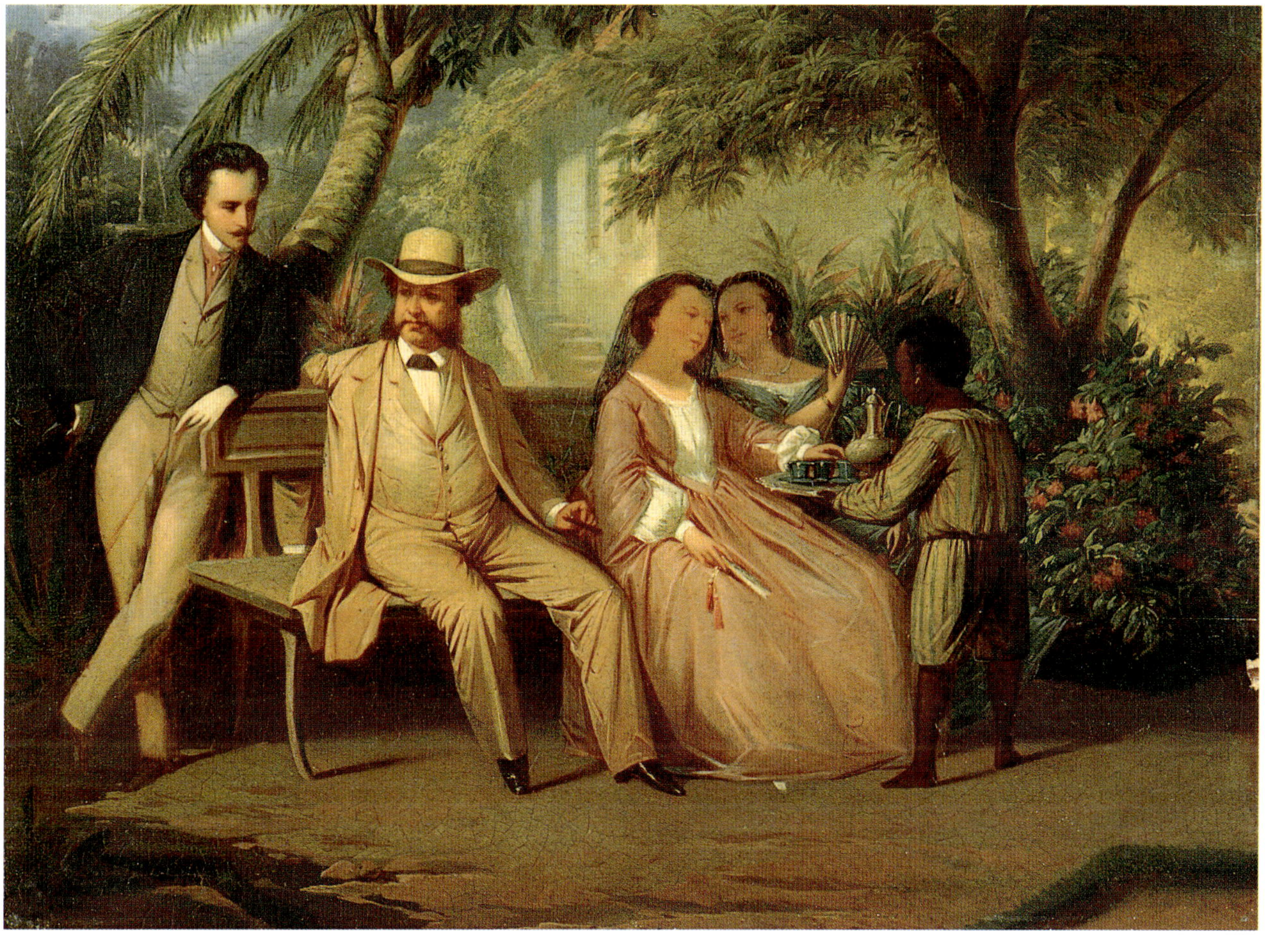

Johann Culverhouse

THE FAMILY OF JOSÉ MARTÍ

Ca. 1880, Oil on panel, 8" x 13"

Gift of Kenneth Worcester Dow and Mary Mohan Dow

ACKNOWLEDGMENTS

Of all of the islands of the Caribbean, Cuba has played the most important role in the development of the United States. From as early as the sixteenth century, this "key to the New World," as Cuba was called, has exerted a powerful influence on the Western Hemisphere, as well. Yet because of a series of unforeseen historical events, North Americans today know little about Cuban culture and the role of the arts in Cuban life. Moreover, since the middle of the twentieth century, millions of exiled Cubans have been removed from the deep and rich roots of their culture. And while a resilient Cubanismo has been successfully transplanted throughout the world, there are few opportunities for Cubans today to celebrate the historic images of this sophisticated Caribbean civilization.

It is a pleasure for the Cuban Foundation to work with a group of partners to publish *Cuba: A History in Art*. This volume records pertinent and often unrecorded information central to an understanding of art created in Cuba and the culture that produced it.

Thanks must be extended to the late F. Ruben Batista and the Cuban Foundation for their miraculous efforts in assembling an impressive core collection of Cuban paintings and decorative arts, many of which are included here. Additional thanks are given to individual donors who have enriched this collection over the last forty years. These donors are included on label information on each work discussed.

Very special thanks are sincerely extended to Juan A. Martínez of Florida International University, a preeminent scholar in the field of modern Cuban art history. His book, *Cuban Art and National Identity: The Vanguardia Painters, 1927–1950* continues to be among the most comprehensive and astute of the new criticism and reappraisals of the role of Cuban art in the modern aesthetic. I would like to acknowledge Professor Martínez's contributions to this volume in both his perceptive essay on the modern period in Cuba and his brief notes on several influential painters. I would like to thank my colleagues at the Colección Ramos for their assistance in this project. Their comprehensive bilingual volume, *Great Masters of Cuban Art*, published by the Museum of Arts and Sciences in Daytona Beach in 2009, contains essays on subjects and themes in Cuban art as well as biographies of artists and a bibliography. This publication adds much to a more complete study and appreciation of Cuban art.

I also thank Stacey G. Sather, David Swoyer, and photographer James Quine for their assistance in the production of this book.

I would also like to thank the Board of Trustees of the Museum of Arts and Sciences, Daytona Beach, and the FBZ Foundation, Miami, for their direct support of the Cuban Foundation Museum.

Final thanks are sincerely extended to fellow Cuban Foundation members Tere Batista, Robert Batista, and Marta Batista Malouf for their lifetime of dedication to the history and culture of Cuba. I dedicate this publication to them.

Gary R. Libby

The Essays and Catalogue

The first essay in this book is a general discussion of the rise of a Cuban style, as European civilization comes to the tropics absorbing African and native Indian influences to produce a heterogeneous New World civilization of great vitality and energy. The colonial period also reflects attitudes about the arts that persist well into the twentieth century when modernism begins to free Cuba from her rich and sophisticated European artistic roots.

The second essay, by Professor Juan A. Martínez of Florida International University, summarizes developments in Cuba as European modernism is reshaped through a new tropical vocabulary. His essay, "Cuban Painting in the Republican Period, 1902–1959," is a perceptive look at the individuals and the forces that came together to create modern Cuban painting.

I have included a brief overview of the development of photography in Cuba from 1839 to 1921, when the flashbulb transformed the medium. Photography was first introduced in Cuba to satisfy commercial interests and needs. It also became an important narrative and artistic medium of significant influence during the 1902 War of Independence and afterward.

Each work of art or group of works by a single artist featured in this publication is accompanied by a brief essay designed to place the work in context. Information on each artist, subject, the art object itself, and the period is presented to help place these rare and significant works of art in a broad cultural, social, aesthetic, and historical context. Each essay is accompanied by a brief bibliography for future reference. In a few instances, little is known about an artist and work of art in the collection. It is our hope that this volume will elicit additional information to better understand the range and variety of Cuban art and artists.

Paintings which are presented in the chronological order of each artist's birthdate. For ease of reference, all works are listed in alphabetical order by artist's surnames under "List of Plates" on page 102. The catalogue authors are Gary Russell Libby (G.R.L.) and Juan A. Martínez (J.A.M.).

Gary R. Libby

Opposite page: Detail, *The Child of the Artist,* Concepción Ferrant.

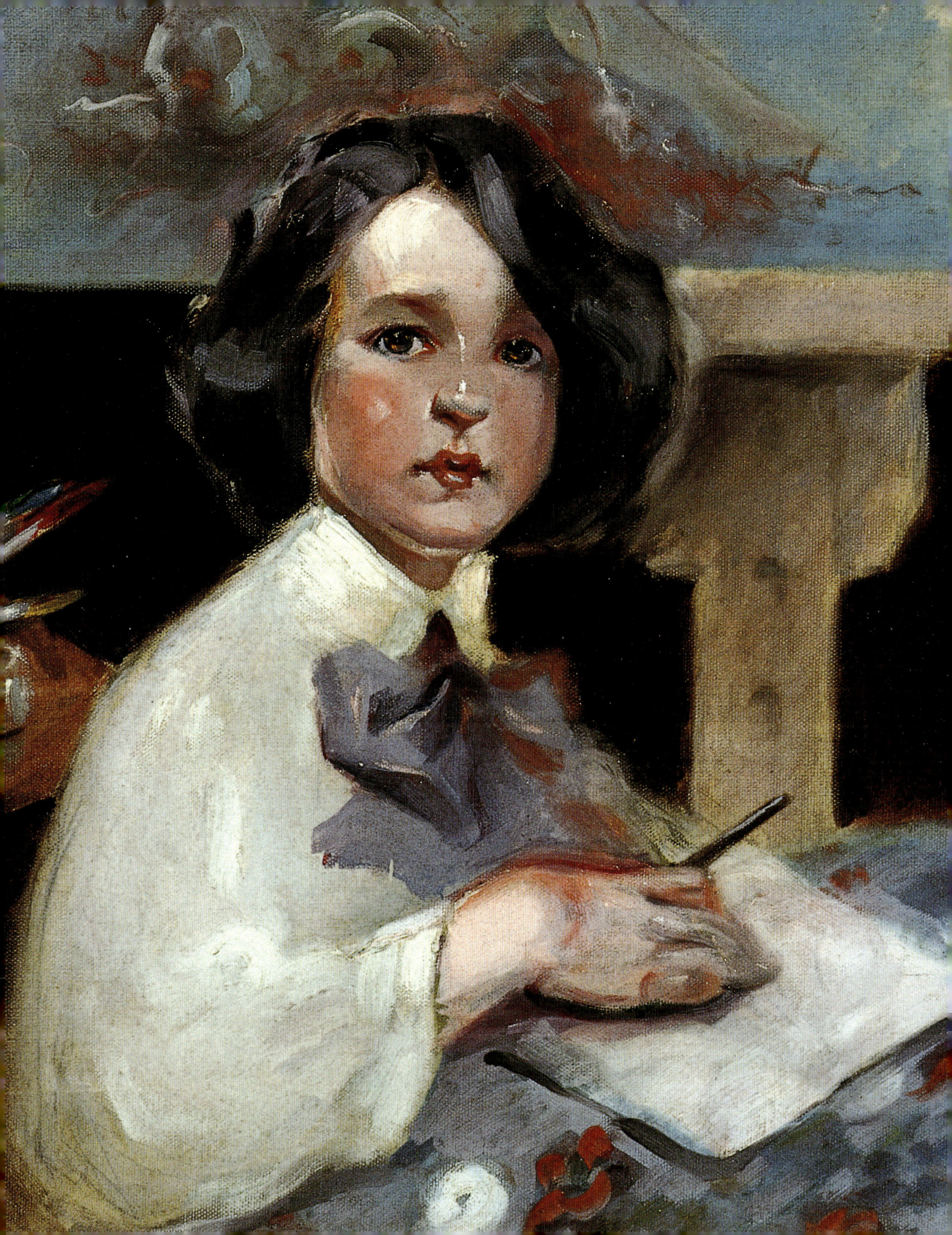

The Rise of a Cuban Style

Gary R. Libby

Before World War II, little was known about the art of Cuba outside of the Latin world. While a few modern painters, including Wifredo Lam, enjoyed an international reputation, most of the academic and modern Cuban masters were unknown.

In 1944, however, everything changed. Alfred Barr, the first director of the Museum of Modern Art in New York, and Cuban art critic José Gómez Sicre brought about a revelation in any understanding of the history of contemporary painting in Latin America when they opened *Modern Cuban Painters* at the new MoMA in April 1944.

In the MoMA *Bulletin* that month, Barr authored a thirteen-page exuberant overview of the exhibition with notes on the participating artists: "The exhibition *Modern Cuban Painters* is limited in size and scope and is entirely unofficial in character. No attempt has been made to present a comprehensive survey of contemporary Cuban painting or a history of its development... I wish to thank Señora Maria Luisa Gómez Meña for her assistance in making the exhibition possible; Señor José Gómez Sicre, who organized the exhibit in Havana; and Señor Jorge Losada, editor of *Norte* for his advice. The selection has been the joint responsibility of Señor Gómez Sicre and the Museum."[1]

Coinciding with the exhibition was the publication of a highly influential softcover book by Gómez Sicre entitled *Pintura Cubana de Hoy*, "a critical analysis and biographical survey of Cuba's modern artists, including a foreword on the history of Cuban painting." Published as a paperback in Havana by Maria Luisa Gómez Meña and distributed in this country by MoMA, it contained 200 pages with 116 plates (20 in full color) and cost $1.75.[2] This book, while praising the accomplishments of the modern artists working in Cuba from 1939 to 1944, also mentions the official academic tradition and some of the folk painters in Cuba, as well as the serious place of the arts in the development of culture on the island. And while many of the pronouncements and opinions expressed by Gómez Sicre seem highly ethnocentric given the temperament of today, they did represent a certain brand of Cubanismo practiced by intellectuals of the 1940s in Cuba.[3]

There is ample proof that the rigorous training of the Academy of San Alejandro and the conservative European traditional view of painting taught there in the nineteenth and early twentieth centuries helped build one of the technical foundations of modern Cuban painting. Cuban naive or folk art established another.[4]

Any understanding of Cuban art must, however, really begin before the sixteenth century when the island became an important naval and commercial center supplying Spanish exploration and development in the New World. The native Taino population of Cuba was decimated by design early in the fifteenth century. Its influence

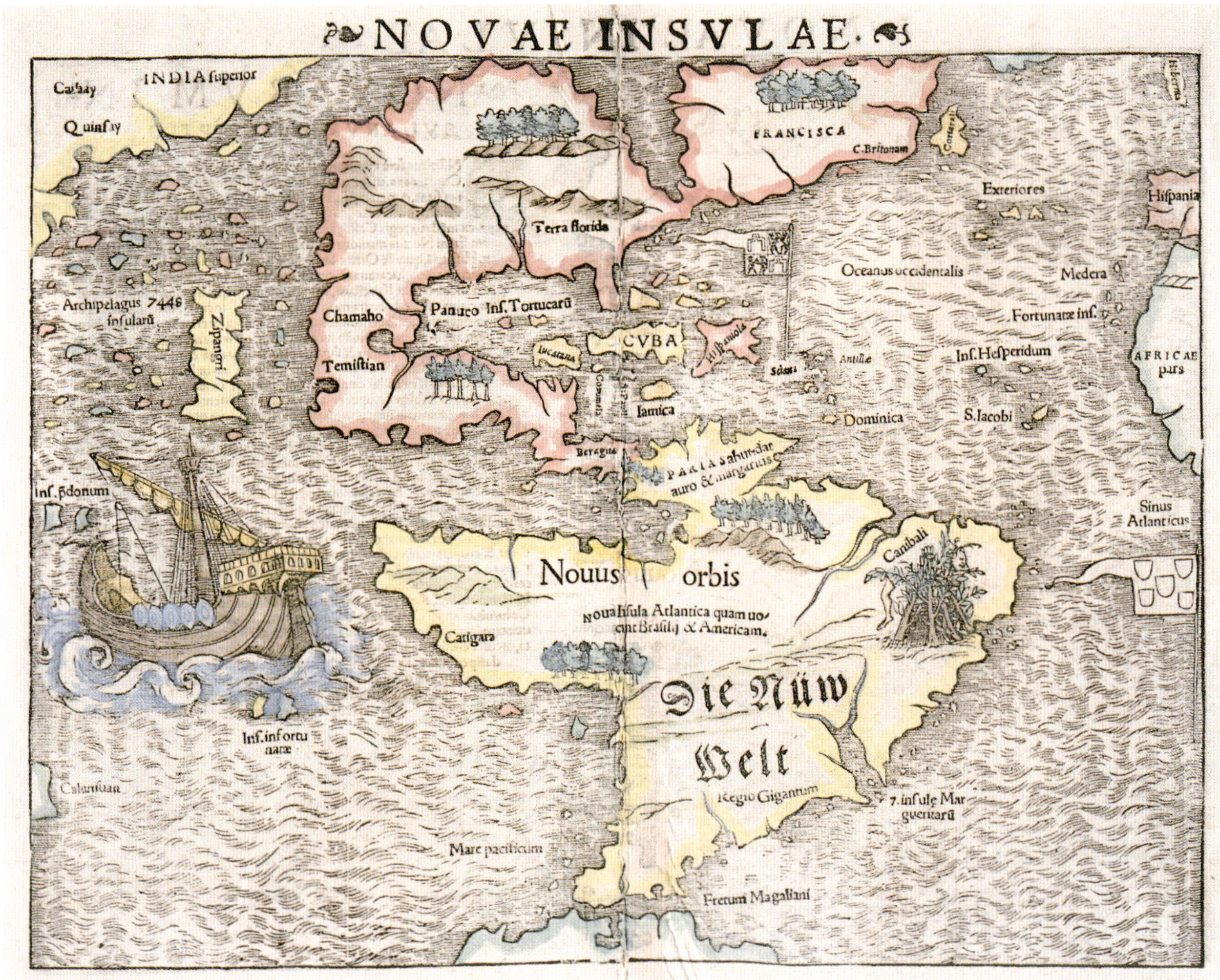

Sebastian Münster (1489–1552) Basle, Map of Novae Insvlae, *From Sebastian Münster, Geographia Universalis, 1540, hand-colored wood engraving, 8" x 11". Gift of Kenneth Worcester Dow and Mary Mohan Dow.*

was to surface two hundred years later in the neo-folk primitivism of modern Cuban painting and the decorative arts, especially ceramics modeled after motifs found on Taino religious objects. The term *Taino* translates as "noble" or "good" in the language of the natives of the Greater Antilles. The Spanish adopted the term *Taino* early in the sixteenth century to distinguish them from the Carib people. It was probably Diego Velazquez de Cuellar, the initiator of the Cuban entrata in 1511, who first described the Taino in a letter to the king dated April 1, 1514. Bartolomé de Las Casas also described the natives of Cuba and attempted to classify them into two major groups. Even the term *Habana* or *Havana* is a Taino word describing a "chieftainship" in western Cuba visited by Velázquez and Narváez.[5]

From the few historical records, and confirmed by recent archaeological investigations, we assume that the Taino lived in villages of several hundred upward to over a thousand individuals. They perfected a well-developed political system with chiefs who were committed to warfare. They were also farmers and fisherfolk who practiced ritual religious activity where images of spirits called "Zemis" were made of cotton, stone, shell, bone, wood, and pottery. It is generally agreed that the arrival of Columbus in 1492 at La Navidad began the steady decline of Taino culture until 1520 when it became extinct.[6] Only after 1927 did Taino art become resurrected as an element in the development of Cuban modernism which absorbed native and African motifs into its new visual vocabulary.

Because of its strategic location, the island of Cuba is clearly represented in maps of Spanish, French, English, Swiss, and Dutch origins as early as the 1540 *Map of Novae Insulae*, from Sebastian Münster's *Geographia Universalis*, printed in Basle.[7] In this hand-colored engraving, Cuba is clearly labeled as CVBA in the Latin-based, first printed map treating the Western Hemisphere as a unit seen at the center of the map between Europe and Africa to the east, and Asia to the west.

Also in the first quarter of the sixteenth century, Giacomo Gastaldi (1500–1565), a Venetian working for that maritime republic, drew his *Isola Cuba Nova,* which was published later in 1561.[8] The map curiously does not show Havana, and longitude is numbered eastward from the prime meridian. In 1611, the Gerhard Mercator (1512–1594) map, called *Cosmographia*, was published in Amsterdam, Holland.[9] This map shows several important Spanish New World islands including Cuba and Havana, which is labeled "most celebrated port of all the West Indies."

By the middle of the seventeenth century, Cuba was accurately delineated and identified as an important geographical location in maps like Jan Jansson's hand-colored engraving *Chart of Insvlae Americanae* from his *Nuevo Atlas* of 1653,[10] and in Johann Baptist Homann's hand-colored engraving *Map of Regni Mexicani seu NOVAE HISPANIAE*, printed in Nuremberg in the early eighteenth century.[11] This latter map is beautifully illustrated by a series of vignettes including one, in the lower left, describing the Spanish losses at the battles of Vigo Bay, 1702, and Cartagena, 1708. These setbacks in the so-called Queen Anne's War forced Spain to suspend the shipping of gold and silver to Europe, causing a panic across the continent, since all currencies were dependent on New World Spanish gold as bullion.

An interesting feature of the Homann map is the strategic importance of Havana in the delineation of the routes taken by homeward-bound Spanish treasure fleets from Cartagena, Colombia, around eastern Cuba to Havana, and from Vera Cruz, Mexico, along the coast to Havana. After reprovisioning in Havana, these fleets traveled north across the Florida Keys, upward along the eastern coast of Florida, and out to sea toward Spain.

Because of the growing importance of Havana as a commercial center for fleets leaving the Americas, by 1780 accurate maps of Cuba were produced by most seafaring European powers. Among the most telling is the Rigobert Bonne (1727–1795) hand-colored and engraved map entitled *L'isle de Cuba* included in the Guillaume Raynal, S. J., *Atlas de toutes les parties connues du Globe,* Geneva, of 1780.[12] Here Bonne describes the main topographical features of Cuba and charts the deep and shallow water around the island through the use of dotted, irregular lines. While no compass rose is included, longitude and latitude are marked, as are Spanish and Castilian leagues.

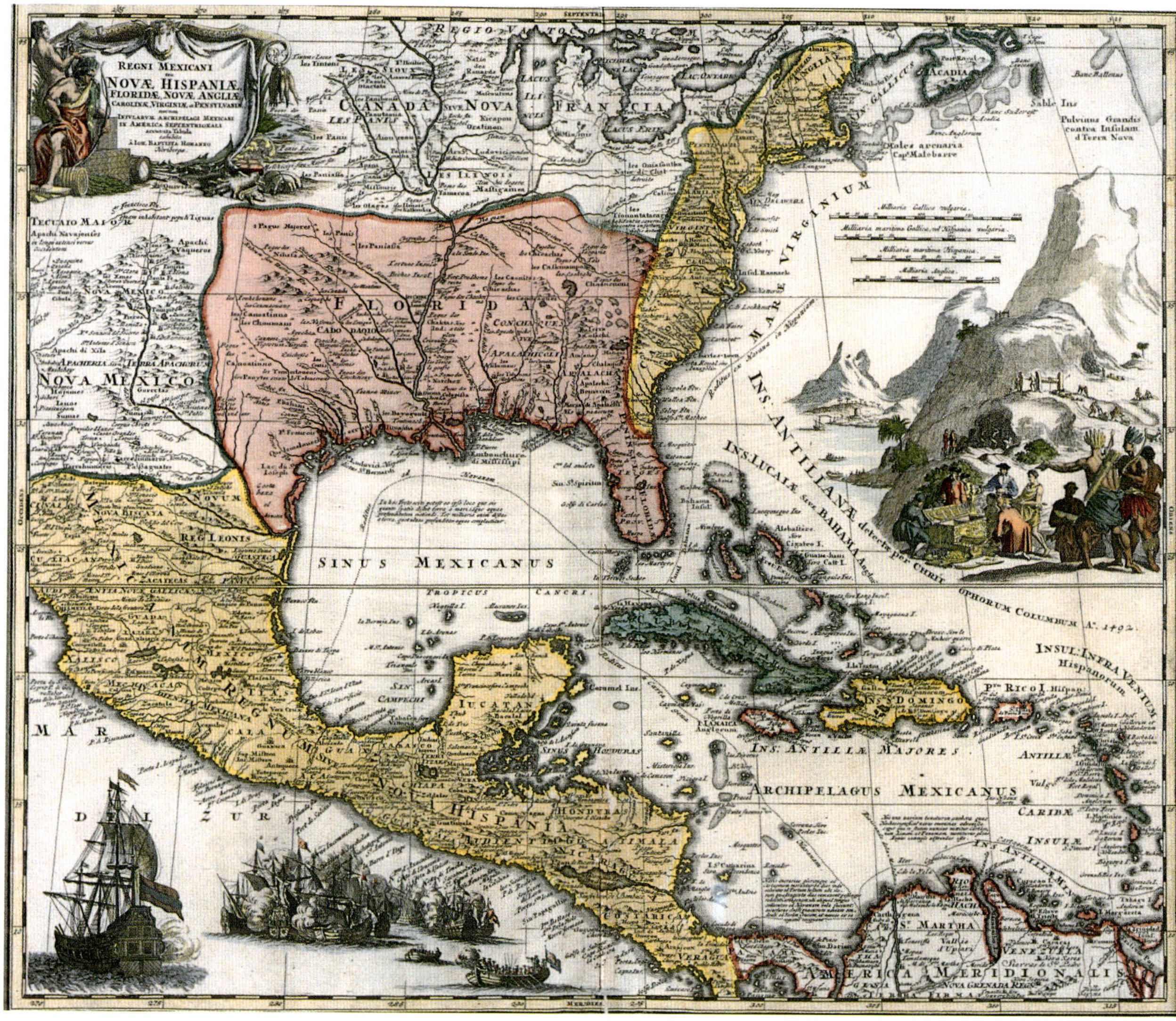

Johann Baptist Homann (1663–1724) Nuremberg, Map of Regni Mexicani seu Novae Hispaniae, *From Johann Baptist Homann, ca. early eighteenth century, hand-colored engraving, 17" x 20". Gift of Kenneth Worcester Dow and Mary Mohan Dow.*

By the eighteenth century, Cuba had moved into an important role in New World Spain. At this time traditional art in the European style came to Cuba.

The first colonial painter to be accurately identified, recorded, and studied was Nicolás de la Escalera (1734–1804).[13] Little is known about de la Escalera, but most scholars agree that he was probably born in Cuba. He restricted his work to naive portraiture and religious painting in the Counter-Reformation Jesuit Baroque style. Often criticized for his limited palette and modest artistic vocabulary, de la Escalera probably used religious carvings as models for his paintings.

At this time, Cuba, as a major commercial center, continued to import objects from the Old World and other New World Spanish possessions. Furniture and porcelain from Europe, silver objects from present-day Colombia and Peru, jewelry from throughout Central America, and furniture and decorative arts from Mexico flowed into Havana and other port cities and through these cities to the Cuban provinces. Featured in this text, a set of four Latino paintings from the eighteenth century also help to illustrate the heterogeneity of the peoples in New World Spain and the roots of some of the exotic racial mixtures found there.

The second recorded Cuban artist of the late eighteenth century was Vicente Escobar (1757–1834), the preeminent portrait painter of the colonial era.[14] With his principal student, Juan del Rio, Escobar established an important studio in Havana for the Cuban aristocracy and for the administrative and rising merchant classes. Joined by a Frenchman, Juan Bautista Vermay (1786–1833), these academic painters introduced the European-inspired formal tradition in Cuban painting, championed by the creation of an officially sanctioned school of art, the Academy of San Alejandro, in 1818. Here the rigorous classicism of Jacques Louis David (1748–1825), Vermay's teacher and friend, helped educate generations of Cuban artists. The academy was established by the order of Spanish Intendente Alejandro Ramirez, who appointed Vermay as the first director. A series of paintings by Vermay centrally located in one of the most important buildings in Cuba, the Templete of Havana, around 1820 helped promote European classicism in Cuba. Another important and contributing influence to the development of a European-inspired conservatism came from Bishop Juan José Diaz de Espada y Landa (1756–1832), a cultured Basque friend of Francisco Goya who came to Havana with a large personal collection of European paintings in the Spanish, French, and Italian styles. Landa was aware of the power of dramatic religious painting and used his collection as a model for the development of artistic taste in Cuba. While apologists for a freer modern Cuban style which appeared after 1927 (the date of the first modern art exhibits in Cuba) often attack the academic beginnings of Cuban art as too narrow and rigid, the Academy of San Alejandro, like its contemporaries in Paris, Madrid, and Rome, helped create a respect for the significance of the arts as serious symbols of a European-inspired national culture, transported to the tropics in Cuba. And while many of the great academic history and narrative painters of the nineteenth and early twentieth centuries represented here are still underappreciated today, they provided the atmosphere, the training, and the studio instruction for most of the modern Cuban painters of the second quarter of the twentieth century, all of whom studied at San Alejandro.

In the second half of the eighteenth century, the Cuban sugar and tobacco industries flourished. Engravers from throughout Europe came to Cuba to help promote them. Of this large group of enterprising artists, Miahle, Barañano, Garneray, and Laplante are the best known and most accomplished. However, Santiago Lessieur y Durand is recorded as the first lithographer working in Cuba. We know he was in Havana in the autumn of 1822. His shop, the Music Lithograph Printer's House, received a patent in 1823. Louis Caire, the second recorded lithographer, arrived from Paris in February 1829. A second shop, Tejada y de Tapia, owned by Juan de Mata, opened in 1839 in Santiago de Cuba. In the spring of 1837, Francisco Miguel Cosnier and Alejandro Moreau de Jonnes opened a third

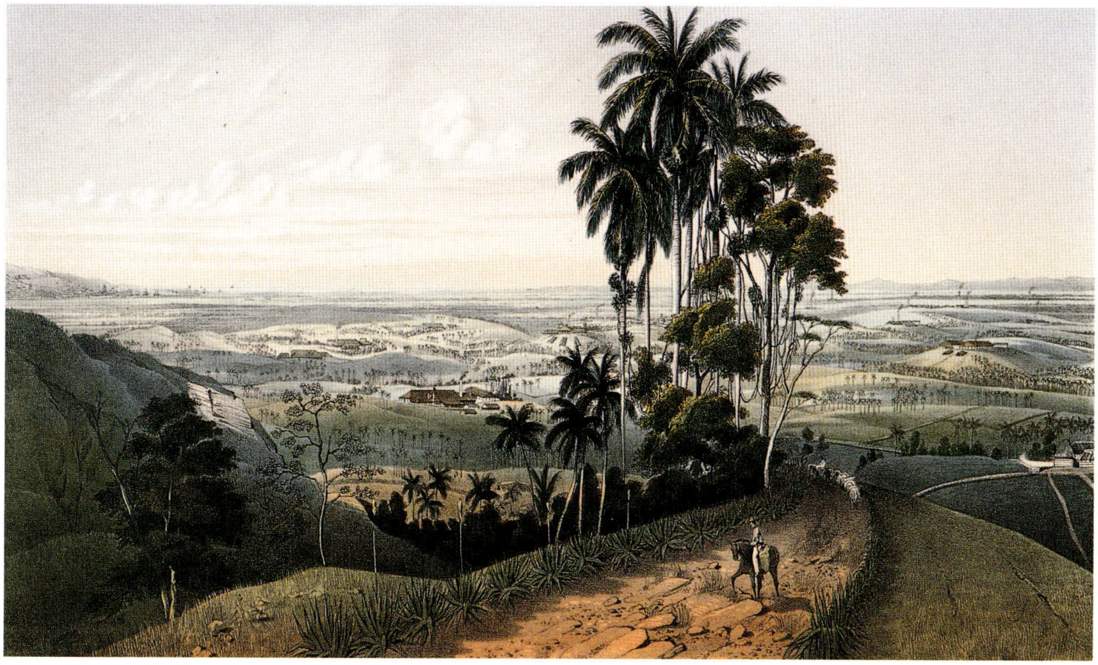

Eduardo Laplante, Valle de la Magdalena, *ca. 1846, Lithograph, 11" x 16". Gift of Marshall Stewart.*

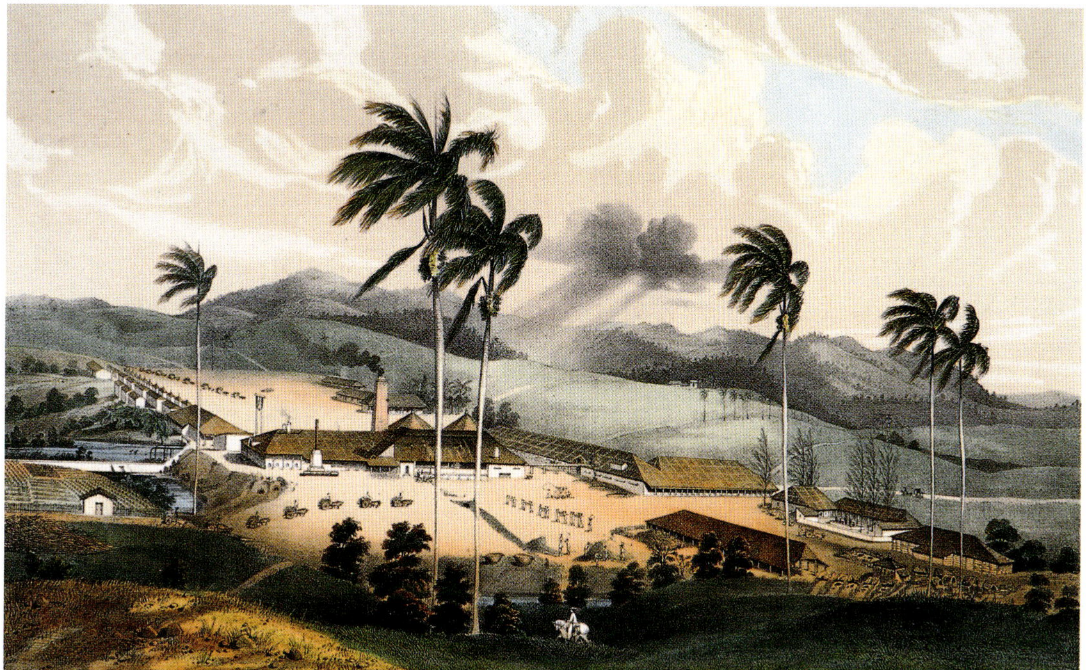

Eduardo Laplante, Ingenio Güinia, *ca. 1846, Lithograph, 11" x 16". Gift of Marshall Stewart.*

printing house. In July 1839, they published a series of landscapes by Frederico Mialhe entitled *The Picturesque Island of Cuba.* Francisco and Fernando de la Costa y Prades, two lithographers from Madrid, also established a large printing house in Havana.

Another Frenchman, Francisco Louis Marquier, arrived in Havana in 1846. His shop produced the two most important suites of lithographs made in Cuba: *Album Californiano,* with illustrations by Francisco Ferran and José Baturone, and *Los Ingenios de Cuba*, with illustrations by Eduardo Laplante. Later Marquier began a series called *The Picturesque Tour of the Island of Cuba*, with illustrations by Miahle. Featured here, *Los Ingenios de Cuba*, a graphic record of the great sugar plantations of the late colonial period and one of the treasures of the Museum of Arts and Sciences in Daytona Beach, is considered among the most beautiful lithographs struck in Cuba.[15] Laplante's *Ingenios* represents a highpoint in the development of the graphic tradition in the New World. Aside from their high degree of technical skill, including clarity of line, coloration, and perspective drawing, the lithographs also function as romantic visual descriptions of life on the great plantations of Cuba. Many reveal intimate details of plantation economy from the fashions and elegant lifestyle of the planters, to the everyday chores of workers. Upon closer scrutiny, many of the lithographs also catalogue with great detail the institution of slavery as practiced in Cuba. Slavery was introduced into Cuba in 1522 to supply labor for agriculture. While slavery was officially abolished in Cuba a decade before Emancipation in the United States, the reliance on labor for sugar and tobacco kept the plantation economy and lifestyle alive well into the twentieth century, when industrialization saw a vast movement of former indentured laborers into the cities and factories of a growing and prosperous Cuba. Taken as a whole, the *Ingenios de Cuba* lithographs, unlike most of the later decorative and commercial lithography produced for the tobacco industry, prefigure much of the rich and varied landscape traditions in Cuban art so ably represented in the paintings of Miguel Arias, Esteban Chartrand, and many academic and modern masters of San Alejandro.

During the rest of the nineteenth century, the Academy continued to attract promising students from throughout Cuba who came to Havana to compete for openings at the school. San Alejandro taught a rigorous curriculum in the basics of realistic and representational art with departments, classes, and examinations in chiaroscuro, anatomy of form, color studies, figure drawing from classical sculpture, and finally drawing and painting from live models. Until 1879, only male students were allowed to study at San Alejandro. Then, under the leadership of painter, teacher, and newly appointed director, Miguel Melero (1836–1907), women were invited to attend as full matriculating students.

In 1902, the first Republic of Cuba was created after a long and difficult war with Spain that was ably captured by a large and growing group of Cuban photographers.[16] And while the political and commercial world in Cuba expanded dramatically with increased international trade and immigration, the official and recognized arts remained a willing captive of conservative Cuban high culture.

At this time a more vigorous academic style based loosely on Spanish formulas was developed at San Alejandro by a group of artists led by

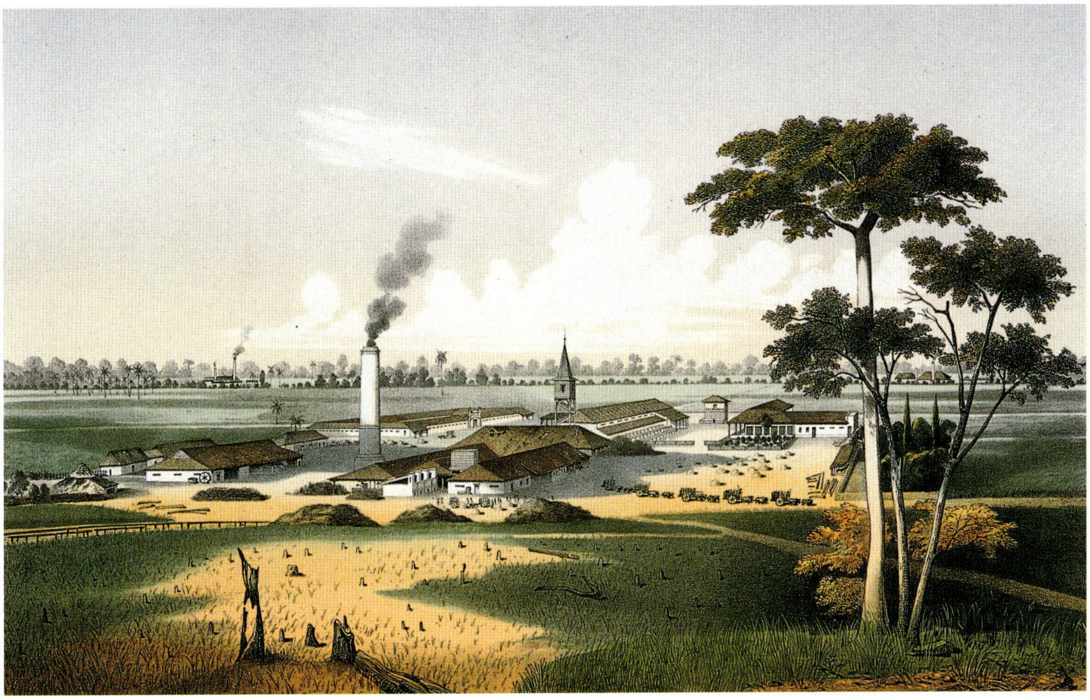

Eduardo Laplante, Ingenio Union, *ca. 1846, Lithograph, 11" x 16". Gift of Marshall Stewart.*

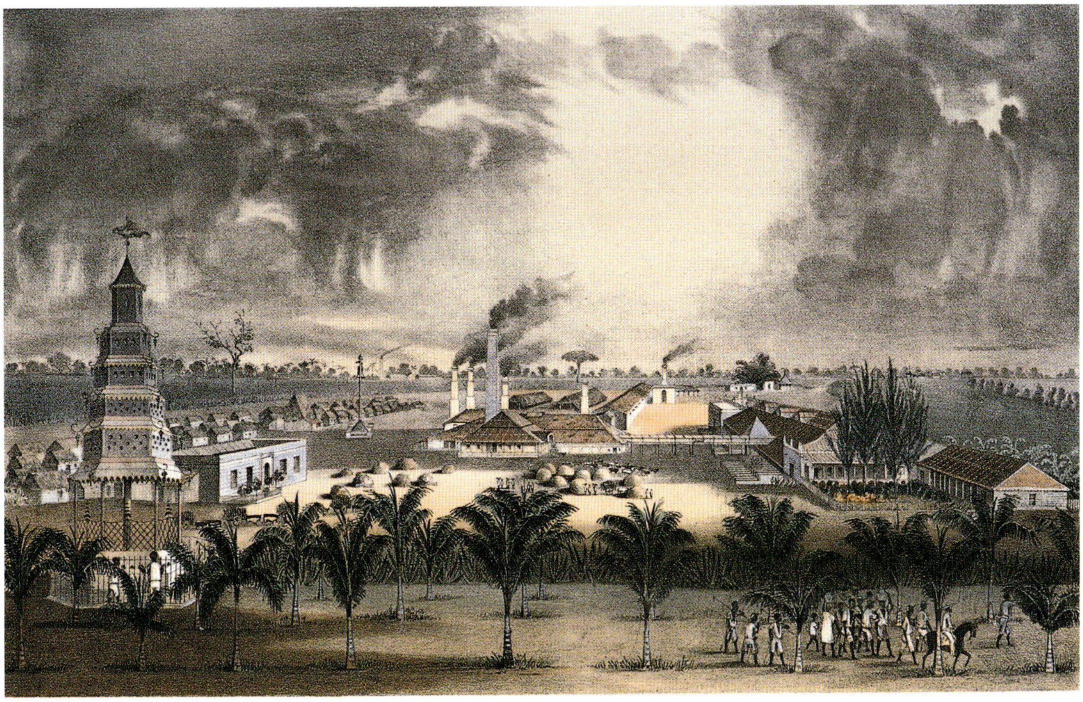

Eduardo Laplante, Ingenio Intrepido, *ca. 1846, Lithograph, 11" x 16." Gift of Marshall Stewart.*

Armando Menocal (1861–1942) and Leopoldo Romañach (1862–1951), called the "last link with the painters of the past generation" by Gómez Sicre. Romañach was aware of the growing wave of modernism in Europe and personally visited early exhibitions of the impressionists and post-impressionists in Paris.[17] However, Romañach continued to extol the more conservative academic approach to art that he learned in Spain, Italy, and France, where he studied with Alexander Cabanel (1824–1889), the master of the new French academic style. Yet Romañach allowed his students to study and discuss the work of Monet, Renoir, Pissarro, and Cézanne, whose works were reproduced in color in magazines of the period. Many of the great modern Cuban painters including Eduardo Abela, Victor Manuel, Antonio Gattorno, Fidelio Ponce de León, and Amelia Peláez studied with Romañach and other professors at the Academy of San Alejandro after 1920.

An important and enlightened element of the curriculum at San Alejandro included scholarships for the best students to study abroad where many of this new generation embraced the developing vocabulary of international modernism.

After 1927, the year of the first serious exhibitions of modern Cuban art in Havana,[18] the Academy of San Alejandro withdrew into the safety and relative obscurity of conservative academic painting as the new modernism from Europe found a rich and varied expression in Cuba.

Gary R. Libby

NOTES

1. For an overview of the exhibition including short selected biographies of included artists, see Alfred Barr, "Modern Cuban Painters," *Museum of Modern Art Bulletin* 11, no. 5 (April 1944): 2–14.

2. Barr: 19.

3. For a personal analysis of early Cuban art history, see José Gómez Sicre, *Pintura Cubana de Hoy* (Havana: Maria Luisa Gómez Mena, 1944).

4. For a study on modern Cuban painting that discusses influences, see Juan A. Martínez, *Cuban Art and National Identity: The Vanguardia Painters, 1927–1950* (Gainesville: University of Florida Press, 1994).

5. For a discussion on archaeological information on the Taino, see William F. Keegan, *The People Who Discovered Columbus: The Prehistory of the Bahamas* (Gainesville: University of Florida Press, 1992), 4–11.

6. For a general discussion of Taino culture, see Jerald T. Milanich and Susan Milbrath, editors, *First Encounters: Spanish Explorations in the Caribbean and the United States, 1492–1570*, Florida Museum of Natural History, (Gainesville: University of Florida Press, 1989), 49–54.

7. For a full discussion of this map, see Peter A. Cowdrey Jr., *Borders of Paradise*, ed. Dana Ste. Claire, (Daytona Beach: The Museum of Arts and Sciences, 1995), 24–25.

8. For a discussion of this map, see Joseph H. Fitzgerald, *Quest for the Indies: Routes of Exploration* (Miami: The Historical Association of Southern Florida, 1992), 71.

9. Ibid. 73.

10. Cowdrey, *Borders of Paradise*, 34–35.

11. Ibid., 38–39.

12. Ibid., 46–47.

13. For a discussion of colonial artists, see Gary R. Libby, *Two Centuries of Cuban Art, 1759–1959* (Sarasota: John and Mable Ringling Museum of Art; Daytona Beach: the Museum of Arts and Sciences, 1980).

14. Gómez Sicre, *Pintura Cubana de Hoy*, 16–18.

15. Ibid., 18.

16. For a discussion of the rise of photography in Cuba, see Gary R. Libby, *Salon and Picturesque Photography in Cuba, 1860–1920* (Daytona Beach: The Museum of Arts and Sciences, 1988).

17. For discussion of the career of Romañach, see *Painting and Sculpture in Cuba* (Havana: Edition of Homage, 1952), 71–80. This publication discusses many of the significant academic painters of San Alejandro.

18. See Martínez, *Cuban Art and National Identity*.

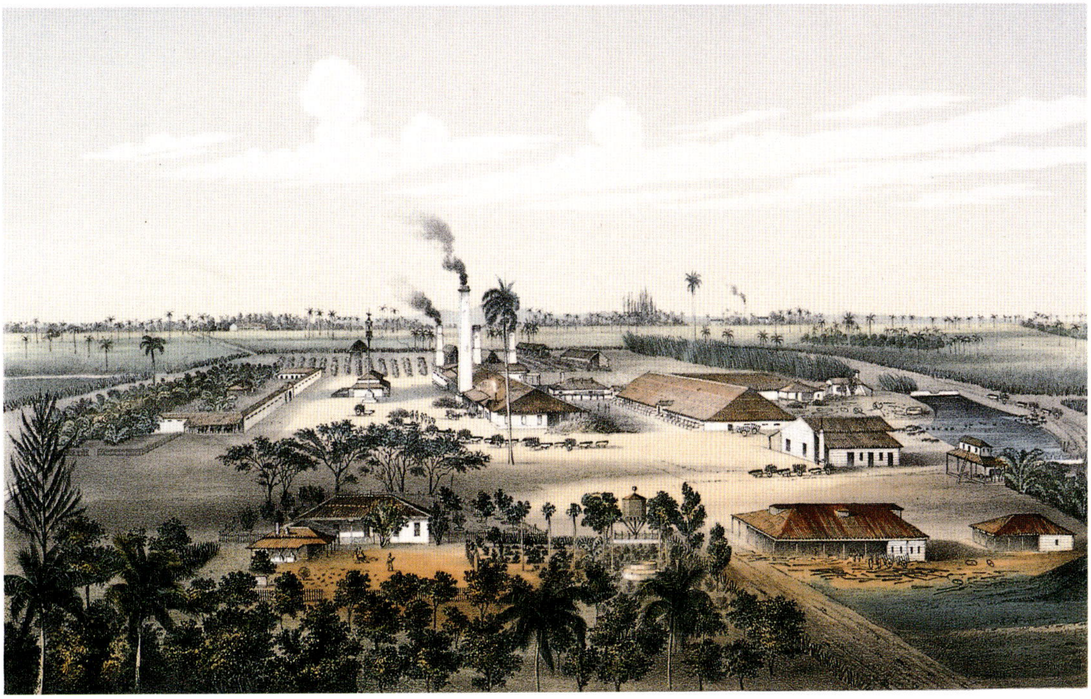

Eduardo Laplante, Ingenio Tinguaro, *ca. 1846, Lithograph, 11" x 16". Gift of Marshall Stewart.*

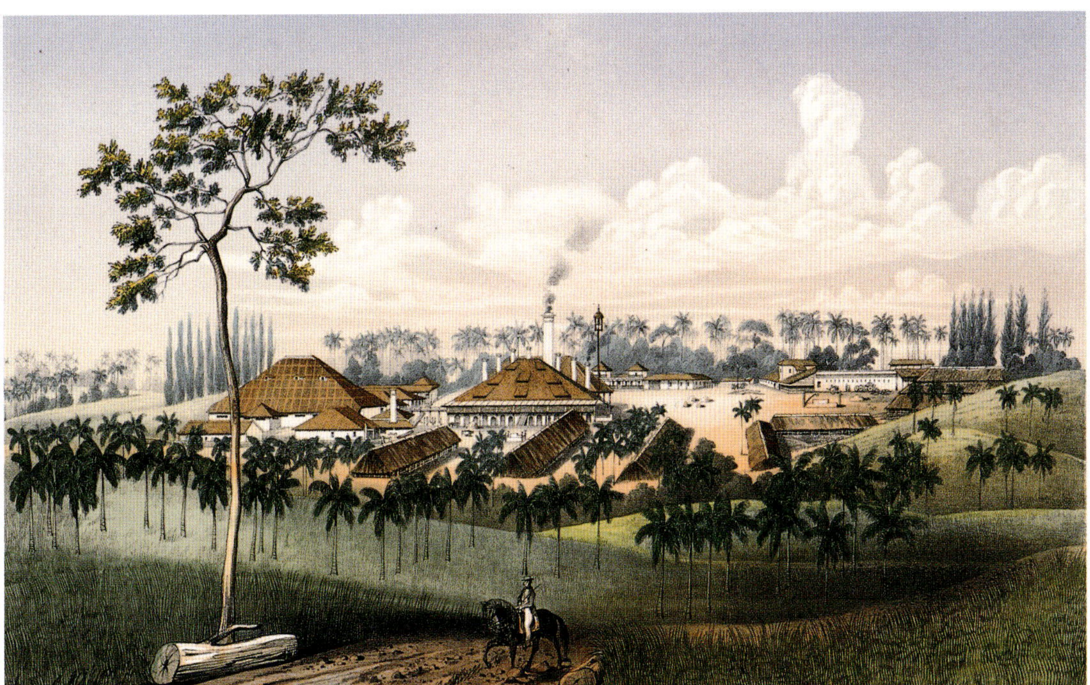

Eduardo Laplante, Ingenio Trinidad, *ca. 1846, Lithograph, 11" x 16". Gift of Marshall Stewart.*

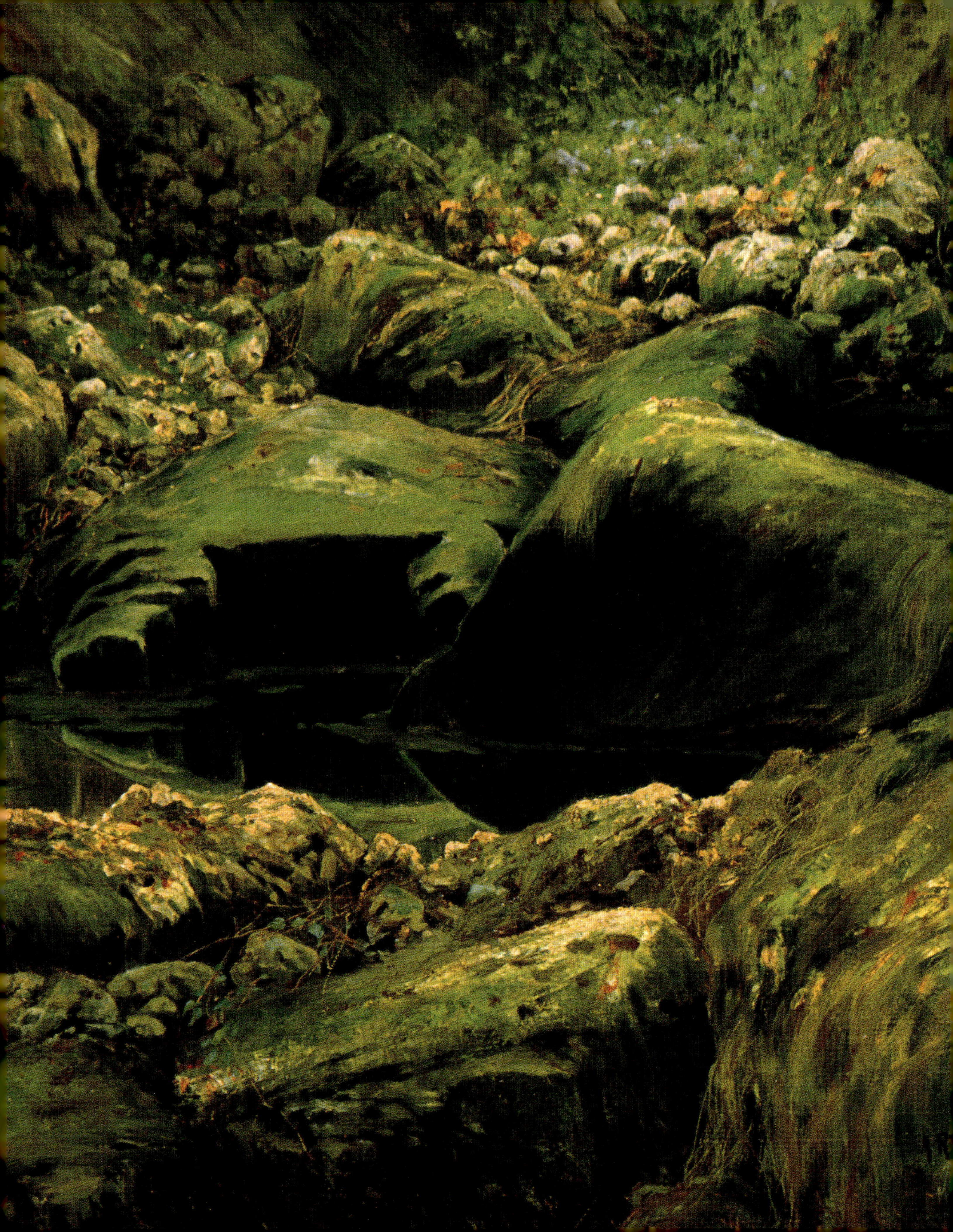

Cuban Painting in the Republican Period, 1902–1959

Juan A. Martínez

The political and the cultural histories of Cuba have unfolded at different paces. The appearance and development of easel painting in Cuba with some indication of a specific sense of place and culture predate Cuban independence from Spain in 1898 and the formation of a republic in 1902. Painting was officially established in Cuba with the opening of a free national school of drawing and painting in 1818, known as the Academy of San Alejandro. This academy of art was instituted by the Spanish authorities (in a colony with a rapidly growing economy and strategic value) to elevate the practice of drawing and painting from a craft to a fine art, thus making it possible for whites to enter what up to then was considered a lowly trade done by blacks and mulattoes. Although San Alejandro fulfilled its purpose, it contributed little to the most important painting done in Cuba in the second half of the nineteenth century, Federico Martínez's portraits of the creole class, Esteban Chartrand's and Gillermo Collazo's "Cuban" landscapes, Armando Menocal's sketches of the war of independence, and the Spaniard Víctor Patricio Landaluze's vernacular scenes. These artists were among the first to use European artistic languages, such as naturalism and romanticism, to represent their natural environment, creole human types, and the island's history. As in the rest of the Americas, the recontextualization of European painting in Cuba began with the subject matter.[1]

The beginning of the new century and the formation of the Cuban republic in 1902 brought mainly institutional changes to the development of Cuban art. San Alejandro took the artistic lead in the first quarter of the century producing a score of professional artists, while academic painting in Cuba found its highest expression in the work of Armando Menocal, Leopoldo Romañach, and Domingo Ramos. Menocal is best remembered as the painter of the second war of independence, whose oil sketches done in the field are the most memorable images of that war in Cuban art. He was also a popular portraitist and an estimable landscape painter. Romañach was a prolific painter and a much loved professor, whose major contributions as an artist were his marines, done in the northern keys of Cuba from the 1920s on. These marines are the first body of paintings to acknowledge the insular nature of Cuba and to capture its light and atmosphere. Ramos's contribution was as a landscape painter with an eye for Cuba's tropical colors. He also discovered, artistically speaking, the Viñales valley in the province of Pinar del Rio. In general, the academic artists worked for Cuba's upper class and the state, fulfilling the

Opposite page: Detail,
Symphony in Green, Antonio Rodriguez Morey

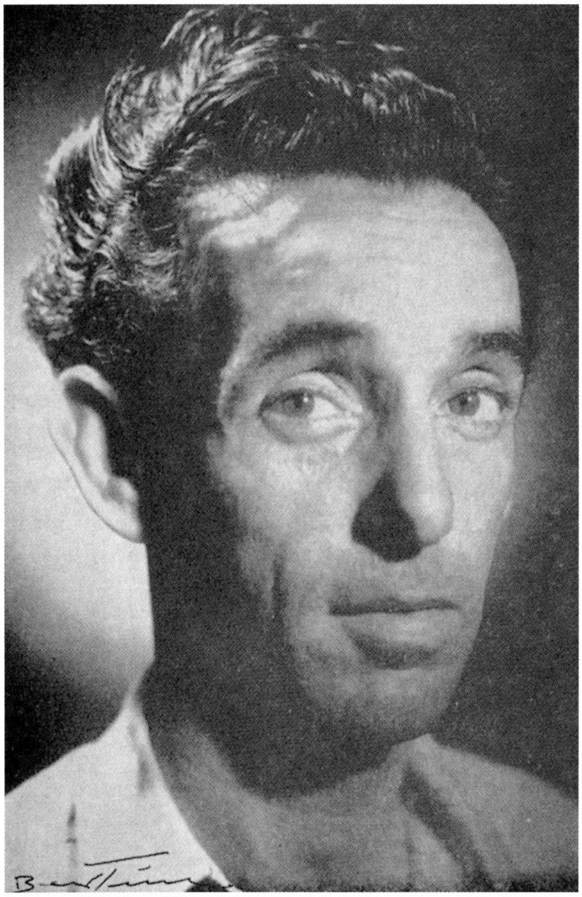

Reproduced from *Pintura Cubana de Hoy*, photograph by Berestein.

Victor Manuel

usual demand for flattering portraits in the case of the former and inspirational patriotic paintings in the case of the latter.

The new status of Cuba as a republic led to the foundation of educational and cultural institutions, such as the National Academy of Arts and Letters and the National Museum of Art. The latter consisted of a historical section and a fine arts section; however, the museum was barely funded and for decades did little to make known Cuba's historical art and did even less to support its living artists. Much more consequential was the foundation in 1916 of the Association of Painters and Sculptors by the painter Federico Edelman Pintó. This association, under the name of Círculo de Bellas Artes, sponsored collective and solo exhibitions of fine arts and caricature, music concerts, and conferences on art and culture. It also released public statements on major issues and events related to the fine arts. For over a decade this association was the main voice and exhibition venue for Cuban artists.

One important missing element was art criticism, which until the late 1930s was practiced by literary figures. The best of these, Julían del Casal and José Martí in the late nineteenth century and Bernardo G. Barros and Jorge Mañach in the early twentieth century, wrote insightful comments on the art of their time. Barros and Mañach published in 1924 and 1928 the first studies on the art of the republic, namely, academic painting up to 1925. By that time a new generation of artists had begun emerging in Havana, bent on challenging academic art.

Like in the rest of Latin America in the 1920s, Cuban artists and intellectuals, inspired by the ideals of European modernism (science, industry, democracy, universal literacy, artistic license, etc.), aimed to change their "backward" societies. At the top of their agenda was cultural renovation. Two related elite groups responsible for reforming Cuba's high culture in the 1920s were the Minority Group and the cultural magazine *Revista de Avance*.[2] The writers, caricaturists, painters, and composers associated with these groups broke with the respective norms in their arts, introducing the ideas and forms of European modernism, to better articulate a sense of self and place. *Revista de Avance* (1927–30) in particular played an important role in the emergence

Opposite page: Detail, *Landscape with Figures,* Victor Manuel.

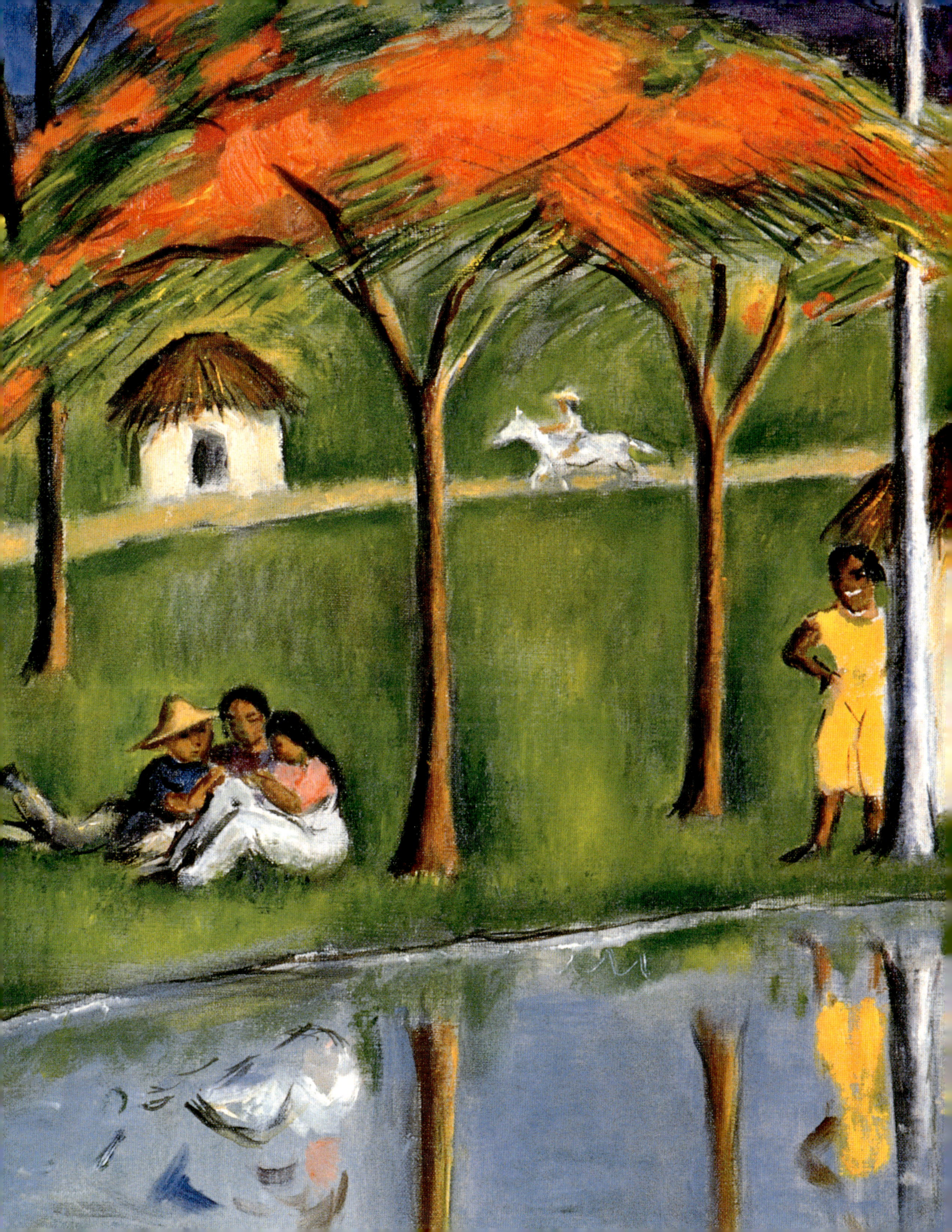

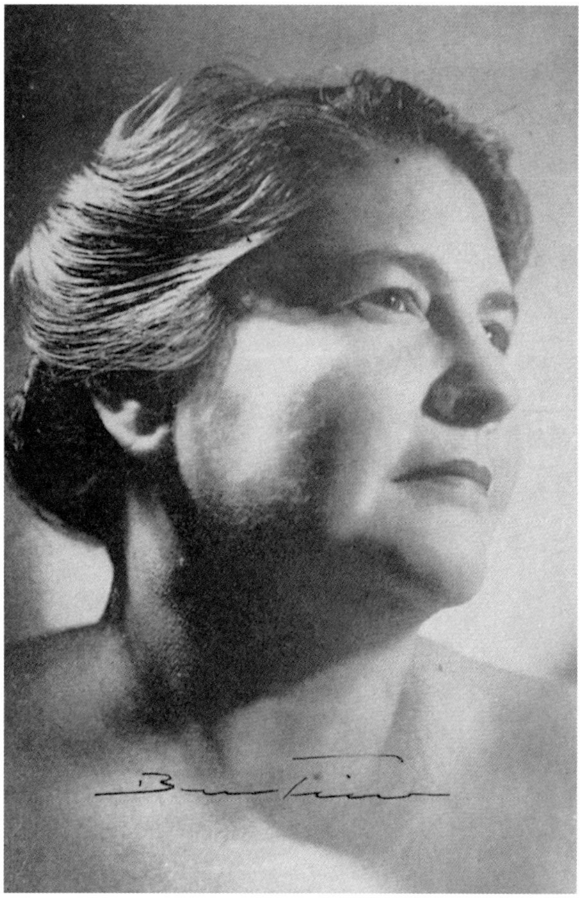

Reproduced from *Pintura Cubana de Hoy*, photograph by Berestein.

Amelia Peláez

of modern Cuban painting. This magazine sponsored the landmark *Exhibition of New Art* in 1927, where the majority of the emerging modernist artists first exhibited together. Moreover it published discourses on the nascent modernist movement in Havana and reproductions of drawings and paintings by the pioneer modernist artists. In fact, the major themes of Cuban modernist painting in the 1930s—the peasant, the Afro-Cuban, and social protest—first appeared in the form of drawings in the pages of *Revista de Avance*.

This first phase of Cuban modernist painting goes into high gear in the early 1930s, when many of the painters of this generation returned to Cuba from their artistic pilgrimage to Paris. In Europe they acquired the conceptual and formal tools to develop their personal artistic languages and visions. The painters of this movement—Eduardo Abela, Jorge Arche, Carlos Enríquez, Arístides Fernández, Antonio Gattorno, Víctor Manuel García, Amelia Peláez, and Fidelio Ponce, among others—adapted European modernist ideas and styles to symbolize a sense of personal identity and a collective sense of place.[3] Using a combination of narrative and symbolism, these painters tried to give voice in Cuban high culture to the most humble and exploited sectors of society—the peasant and the Afro-Cuban. Victor Manuel, Gattorno, and Romero Arciaga approached their subject from a primitivist point of view, strongly influenced by the work of Paul Gauguin. They symbolized the *guajiro* or peasant as simple, languid, and sensual, living in a timeless, uncomplicated, and tropical paradise. In contrast, painters like Enríquez and Fernández took a critical look at the Cuban countryside showing the dire economic and social situation of the *guajiro*. These artists also discovered in the figure of the Afro-Cuban a potent symbol of Cuban identity. For the most part they represented Afro-Cubans as energetic, sensuous, and inclined to magic and ritual. Primitivist stereotypes aside, their representations of Afro-Cubans and their popular culture affirmed a long ignored and integral part of that which is Cuban.

This initial stage of modernism in Cuban art received a measure of support by new institutions. In 1929 a group of civic-minded women founded the Lyceum, a non-profit organization meant to enhance Havana's high culture through art exhibitions, concerts, recitals, conferences, and a circulating library.[4]

Opposite page: Detail, *Still Life*, Amelia Peláez.

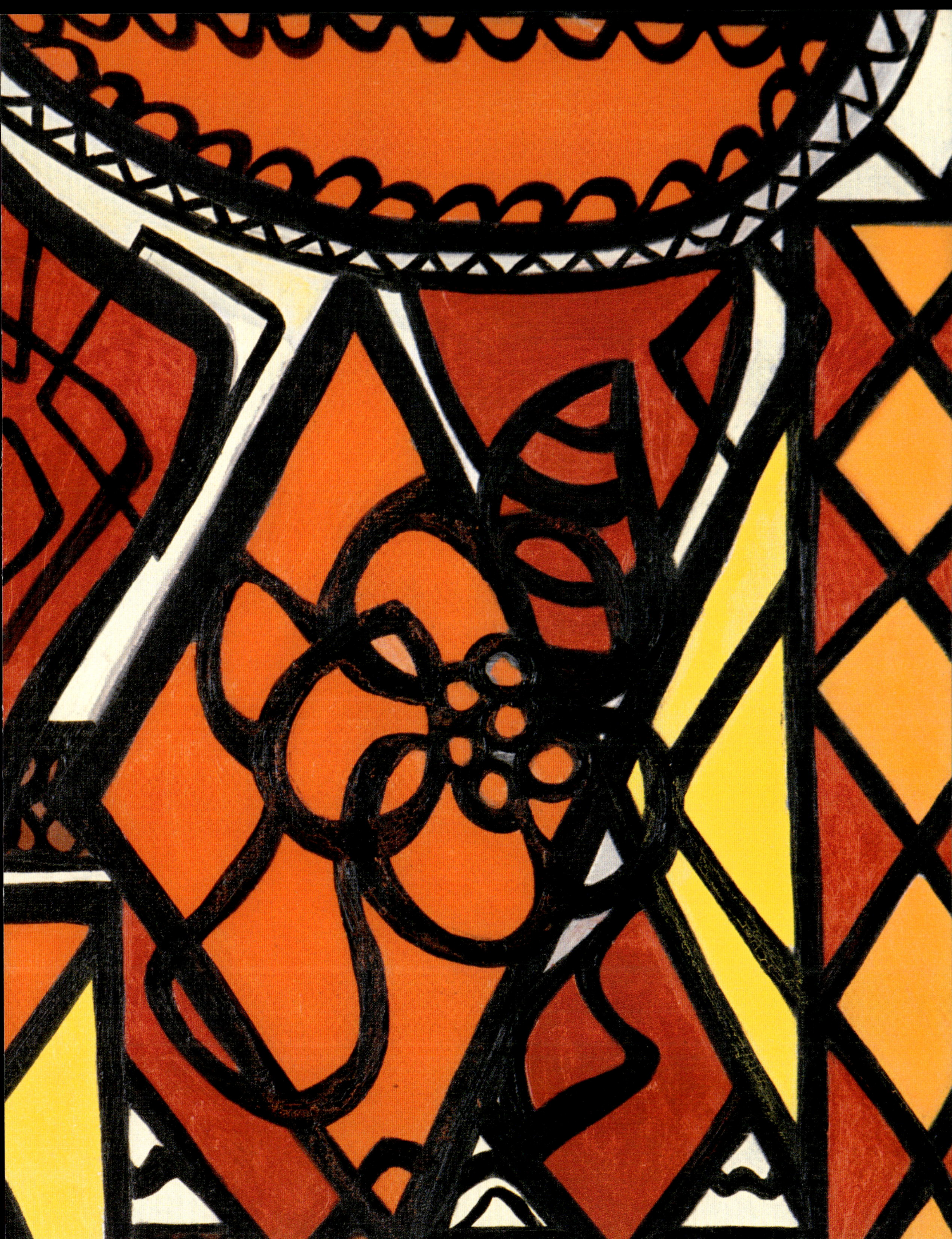

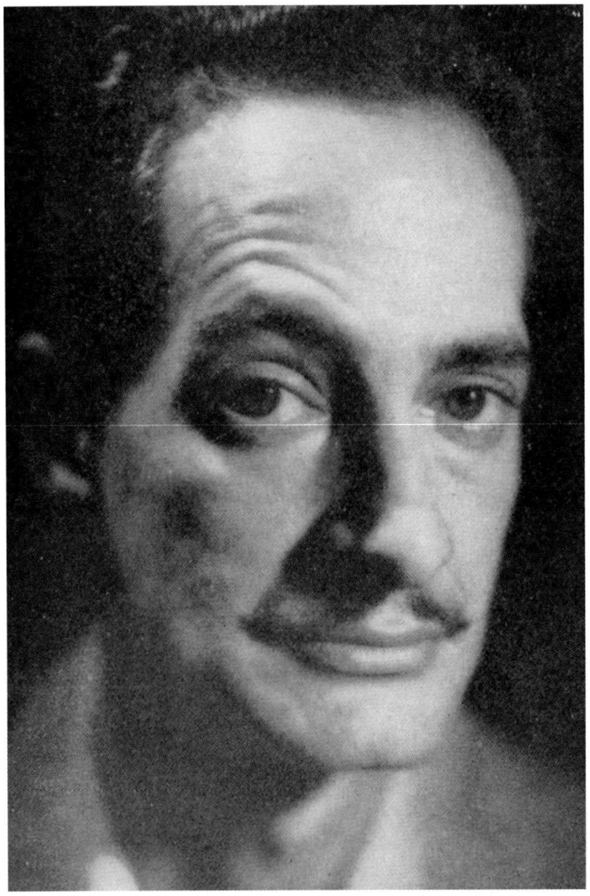

Reproduced from *Pintura Cubana de Hoy*, photograph by Berestein.

Carlos Enríquez

The Lyceum immediately became the main exhibition venue for modernist painting in the 1930s. Modernist painting also benefited from the government's creation of the Directory of Culture as a branch of the Ministry of Education. This office funded for a brief period of time in 1937 a free studio of art, directed and taught by modernist artists with a student body made up of Havana's working class. More lasting in its consequences was the Directory's organization of the First and Second National Salons of Painting and Sculpture in 1935 and 1938, respectively. These salons not only convened a large number of academic and modernist artists, but they also provided purchase awards for works of art which are considered today among the most important paintings in the collection of Cuba's National Museum.[5] While exhibitions of art increased in Havana during the 1930s, art criticism continued to lag behind. By the end of the decade, however, Guy Pérez Cisneros, the first bona fide art historian and critic of Cuban art, made his appearance with publications in various magazines, like *Verbum*, *Selecta*, and *Grafos*.

The political turbulence and depressed economy of the 1930s gave way to a more hopeful decade, which began with a new constitution and free elections. While World War II was ravaging large parts of the globe, Cuba was enjoying a period of relative political stability and economic prosperity. Contrary to the previous decade when modernist painting came into its own against all odds, the visual arts in the 1940s thrived with the help of increased institutional support and the benefit of a decade of modernist painting in the island. The 1940s generation of modernist painters—Wifredo Lam, Mario Carreño, Rene Portocarrero, Mariano Rodríguez, Cundo Bermudez, Mirta Cerra, and Roberto Diago, among others—built on the art of their immediate predecessors, while developing a more mundane, dionysian, and symbolic vision of self and nation.[6]

Visually, they developed a monumental and volumetric approach to form, and they also brightened their palette considerably. Monumentality of form gave a certain transcendental quality to their mundane subject matter, while their bright palette aimed to parallel the intensity of tropical colors. Whereas most of the artists of the first modernist wave visited Paris in their formative years and gravitated to a varied gamut of movements and artistic languages, those of the second generation visited Mexico City or stayed home during their apprenticeship and were strongly influenced by Pablo Picasso's *Suite Vollard* drawings. In 1942, the Lyceum had a Picasso show, which may account in part for his influence on Cuban art at that moment.[7] Overall, these painters developed personal versions of figurative expressionism with an accent on strongly saturated hues.

Like their predecessors, these artists continued to favor an expressive content in art signifying aspects of personal and collective identity. The previous generation's interest in the themes of the peasant and the Afro-Cuban, often loaded with social and political implications, were replaced by the artists of the 1940s with a preference for urban motifs, inspired by the city of Havana. Preceded by Peláez, leading painters of the 1940s, including Portocarrero, Carreño, and Bermudez, affirmed Cuba's Spanish heritage through the use of motifs based on Havana's Spanish colonial architecture, its ornamentation, and a Cuban version of baroque composition. Their 1940s paintings of Havana interiors stand among the most aesthetically rich and idealized constructions of a cultural ethos in the art of Cuba. During that decade the representation of the "Cuban" landscape was not totally abandoned. Mariano's paintings of roosters, Carreño's marines and peasant scenes, Portocarrero's 1944 series of landscapes inspired by the Viñales valley, and Lam's sugar cane fields turned into jungles are major contributions to the perennial representation of the Cuban countryside.

Paradoxically, the most important pictorial expression of the African element in Cuban culture took form in the 1940s, when the Afro-Cuban movement in literature and art had run its course. Lam, whose Cuban production dates mostly to the 1940s, developed during that decade a new and assertive vision of the African presence in the Caribbean. In his paintings of that time, monumental hybrid figures, masks, signs referring to Afro-Cuban deities, the stalks of sugar cane, and tobacco leafs, embodied in the language of cubism and the theories of surrealism, aggressively suggest the persistence of African traditions in Cuba.

The modernist artists of that decade were supported by a nascent cultural infrastructure. Their strongest support still came from the

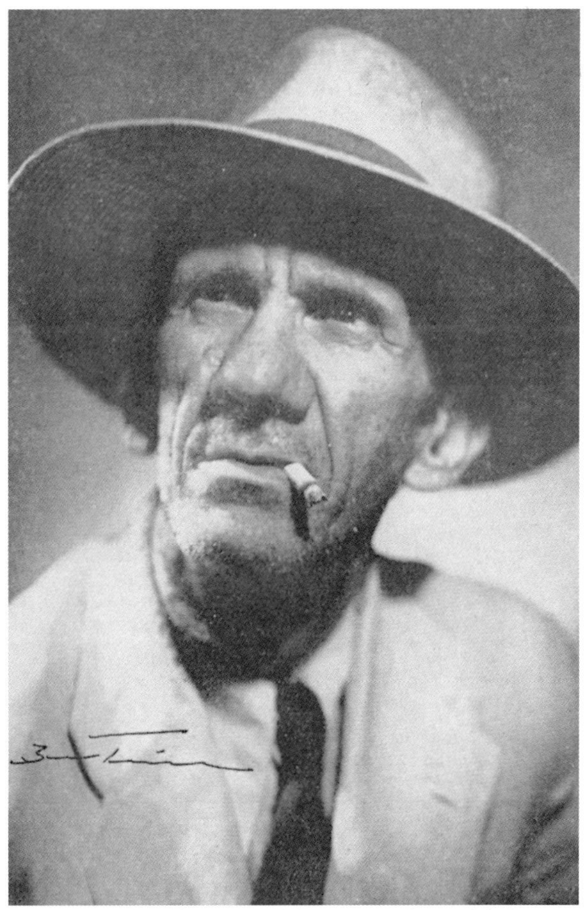

Reproduced from *Pintura Cubana de Hoy*, photograph by Berestein.

Fidelio Ponce

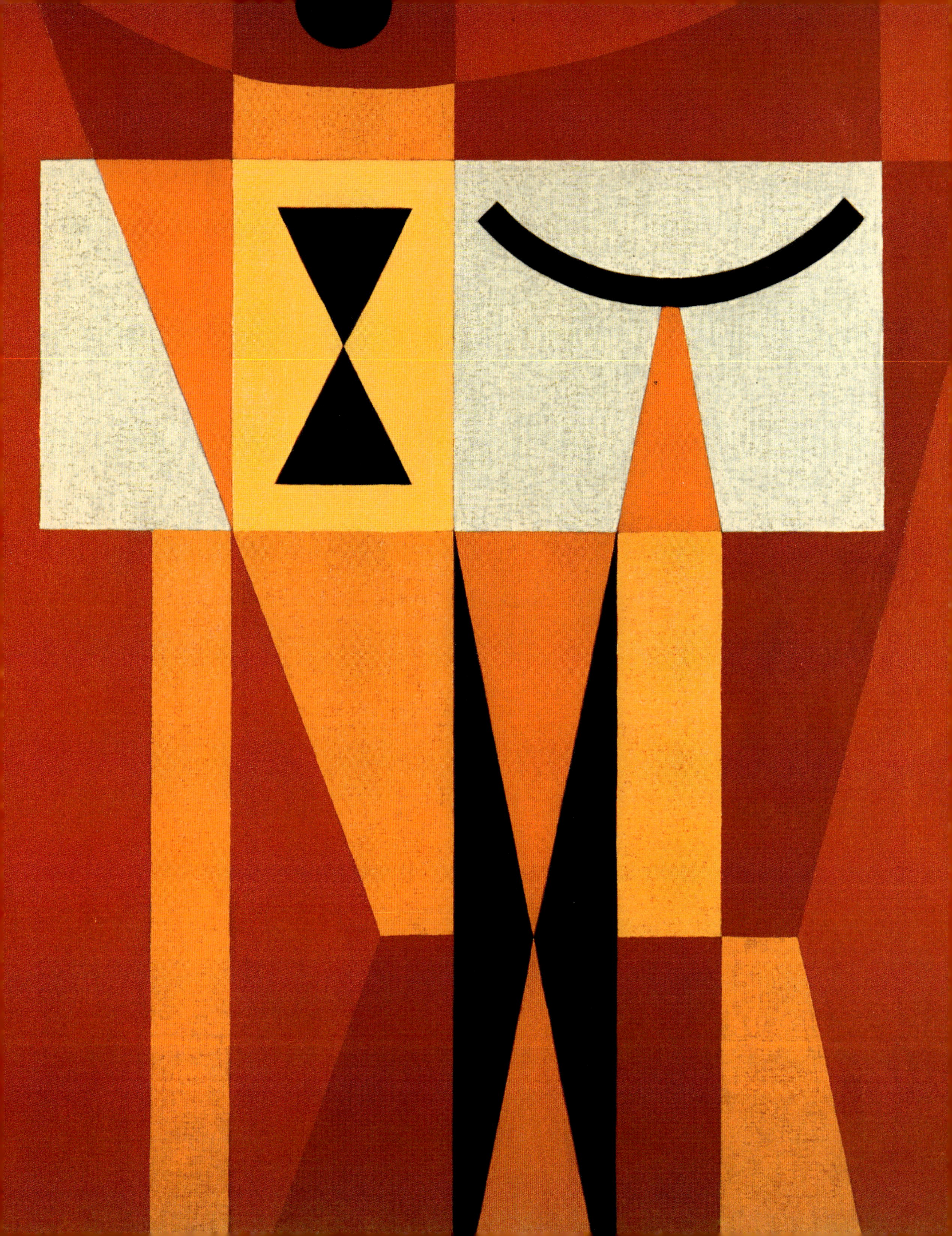

Cuban intelligentsia and professional middle class, who were its public and collectors. Some of these artists, like Mariano and Portocarrero, were closely associated with the group magazine *Origenes*, whose leader, José Lezama Lima, was one of the major ideologists of that generation. A friend and collaborator with Lezama's magazines was the aforementioned art historian Pérez Cisneros, who became a leading critic of the 1940s generation of artists. The art critic and later museum director José Gómez Sicre was also an important promoter of many of the Cuban artists who emerged in the 1940s. These individuals and a few other art historians, critics, and artists were able to channel a minimum of public and private resources to the visual arts.

At the state level, the National Institute of Fine Arts, founded in 1939, sponsored major exhibitions of historical and contemporary Cuban art as well as national salons of fine art during the 1940s and 1950s. Of these exhibitions, *Three Hundred Years of Art in Cuba* (1940) stands out for offering the first survey of Cuban art and thus opening the eyes of contemporary artists to the fact that they had an artistic past. Organizations like the Cuban Commission of Intellectual Cooperation also organized important exhibitions of contemporary art with accompanying catalogues. On the private or civic sector, the Lyceum continued to be a main venue for the exhibition and discussion of modernist art. In 1942 this institution exhibited for the first time in Cuba the works of Picasso, Henri Toulouse-Lautrec, Joan Miró, and Raoul Dufy. The 1940s also witnessed the first attempt to open a professional private art gallery specializing in modernist art, Galería del Prado (1943–44). Its owner, Maria Luisa Gómez Meña, and its director, Gómez Sicre, were instrumental in the organization of the renowned *Modern Cuban Painters* exhibition at the Museum of Modern Art in New York and were responsible for one of the classic books on modernist Cuban art, *Pintura Cubana de Hoy* (1944). All of these resources helped to make Cuban painting, particularly the modernist movement, known in Havana and, for the first time, outside of Cuba. State and private initiatives during the 1940s took Cuban painting, in the form of collective exhibitions, to New York, Washington, D.C., San Francisco, Moscow, Mexico City, La Plata (Argentina), Guatemala City, and Port-au-Prince (Haiti).

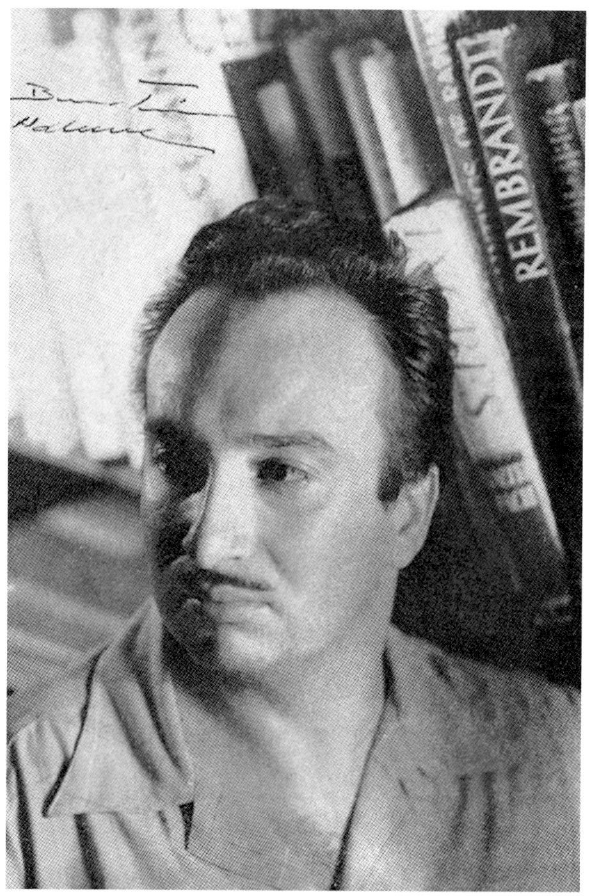

Reproduced from *Pintura Cubana de Hoy*, photograph by Berestein.

Mario Carreño

Opposite page: Detail, *Setting Sun,* Mario Carreño.

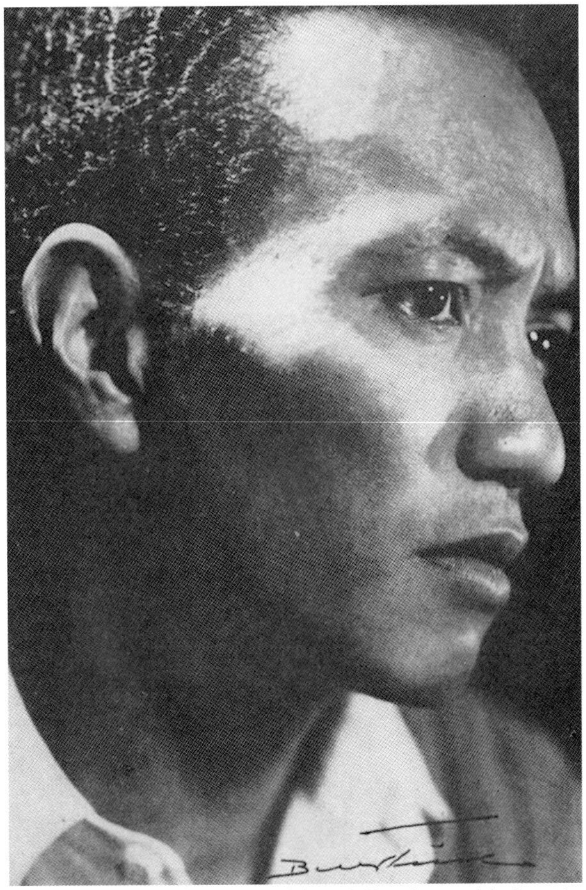

Reproduced from *Pintura Cubana de Hoy*, photograph by Berestein.

Wifredo Lam

The end of the 1940s closed a chapter in Cuban art. In the following decade, Cuban painters in tune with international artistic trends and their own personal and national circumstances took a turn toward abstraction. The 1950s generation of artists reacted against the figurative and symbolic art of their predecessors and against their "regionalism." Armed with the knowledge of the latest vanguard art movements in New York and Paris after World War II, namely abstract expressionism and informalism, the 1950s generation of Cuban abstract artists aimed for a "universal" expression in art. The trend toward abstraction, however, is also connected to developments in Cuba. Twenty years of a nationalist rhetoric in art was wearing thin and political turbulence, which began with a military coup of the right in 1952 and ended with a full-fledged leftist revolution in 1959, seems to have encouraged artists during that decade to look within rather than at the nation in their art.

The 1950s generation of modernist artists were quite varied in their approach to abstraction. Some adapted the vocabulary of cubism, many that of abstract expressionism, and still others that of concrete art. Probably the most important artistic development of that decade was the formation of the group known as Los Once (The Eleven, 1953–54). Its leading members—the painters Guido Llinás, Hugo Consuegra, Raúl Martínez, Antonio Vidal, and Fayad Jamis and the sculptors Tomás Oliva and Agustín Cárdenas—introduced in Cuba the practice of art as an autonomous aesthetic object, beyond narration and symbolism, but with a strong emotional content.[8] Their approximation to New York and abstract expressionism came at a time when North American influence in Latin America was finally reaching beyond economics and politics into the cultural arena. Like in the case of their predecessors, the members of Los Once selectively appropriated elements of their artistic model(s) to construct highly personal visions. Llinás, Vidal, Jamis, and Martínez adapted the New York School's concept of action painting, while using a smaller format, less aggressive application of paint, and a more poetic content. Consuegra's paintings were more consciously constructed and carried evocative titles.

Later another abstract group emerged in Havana following the tenets of concrete art. Its leading members—Sandu Darie, Luis Martínez Pedro, Loló Soldevilla, José M. Mijares, and Rafael Soriano—were concerned with the expression, through geometric abstraction, of universal utopian ideals based on construction, purity of form, and above all, rationality.

The majority of the artists who emerged in the 1950s did not readily adopt abstract expressionism or concrete art as their model. Mijares (early 1950s), Osvaldo Gutierrez, Agustín Fernández, Raúl Milían, José I. Bermudez, Jorge Camacho, and others remained attached to the human figure and/or objects. Many of them followed in the footsteps of the first and second generations by appropriating the formal vocabulary of early modern European art to express, in a more ambiguous fashion than their predecessors, a Cuban presence in their art.

The different generations and groups of Cuban artists working in Havana in the 1950s were supported by a growing but still fragile infrastructure. The Academy of San Alejandro continued to be Cuba's only official art school, and the Círculo de Bellas Artes the forum for academic art. Finally, the National Museum was given an adequate and permanent building in the center of Havana, becoming the seat of the national salons of art and numerous other exhibitions. Non-profit cultural organizations like the Lyceum and Sociedad Cultural Nuestro Tiempo, the latter founded in 1950, continued to play an important role in Havana's cultural life and specifically in the development of the visual arts.[9] During that decade a few commercial galleries—La Habana, La Rampa, Color Azul—also emerged in Havana, yet most had a brief existence. Collectors continued to be an elite within the Cuban middle class and North Americans, who came into contact with Cuban art as tourists in Havana or in exhibitions in the United States. Although this generation of artists had their share of literary friends and art journalists who interpreted and supported their art, no art historian or critic of the stature of a Pérez Cisneros or Gómez Sicre emerged during the 1950s to define and champion their art.[10]

Easel painting in Cuba reached its highest manifestation between the foundation of the republic in 1902 and the revolutionary takeover by the 26 of July movement in 1959. Before 1902 (actually, into the 1920s) painting in Cuba remained far behind the achievements of literature and music, and since 1959 it has lost

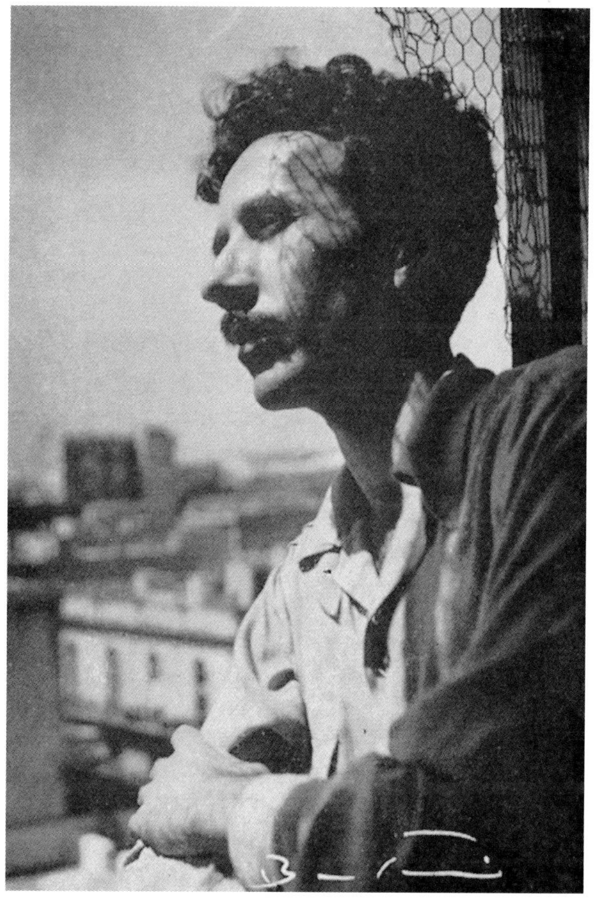

Reproduced from *Pintura Cubana de Hoy*, photograph by Berestein.

Mariano Rodríguez

ground to photography, poster, mixed-media, and installation art. This period, which actually begins in the 1920s and lasts into the early 1960s, is highly dynamic and characterized by a movement from academic to abstract art, from the adaptation of European artistic models to North American ones, and from the representation of a collective-oriented subject matter to the making of introspective signs. One constant in the shifts and changes of modernist Cuban art during the republican period, and for that matter thereafter, is its tendency (paraphrasing from Juan Marinello) to look at the national (Spanish-African-Chinese) with international (Mexican, French, Italian, and North American) eyes, and vice versa.

Although there are magnificent collections of Cuban painting from the republican period in the United States, these are mostly private or, like in the case of the Museum of Modern Art in New York, they are in storage. One exception is the Cuban Foundation Collection of the Daytona Beach Museum of Arts and Sciences, which includes fine examples of academic and modernist paintings. Romañach's *Italian Peasant*, Menocal's *Peasant Child*, and J. A. Bencomo Mena's *Keeper of the Roosters* stand out among the academic offerings. J. Gil Garcia's *Avocado Pears* is an excellent example of that Spanish painter's still lifes, which were immensely popular among the Cuban middle class of the 1920s. The modernist movement is well represented with Victor Manuel's *Landscape with Figures*, Lorenzo Romero Arciaga's *The Cup of Coffee*, Carlos Enríquez's *Harlequins*, Eduardo Abela's *Promenade*, Daniel Serra-Badue's *Cuban Sweets*, Rene Portocarrero's *Figure in Grey*, Amelia Peláez's *Still Life*, Mario Carreño's *Setting Sun*, Mirta Cerra's *Ships*, Guido LLinás's *Composition*, and Darié's *Dynamic Spatial Composition*. As the only permanent public exhibition of colonial and republican Cuban art in this country, the Daytona Beach Museum's Cuban Foundation Collection is a Florida cultural landmark and treasure.

Juan A. Martínez

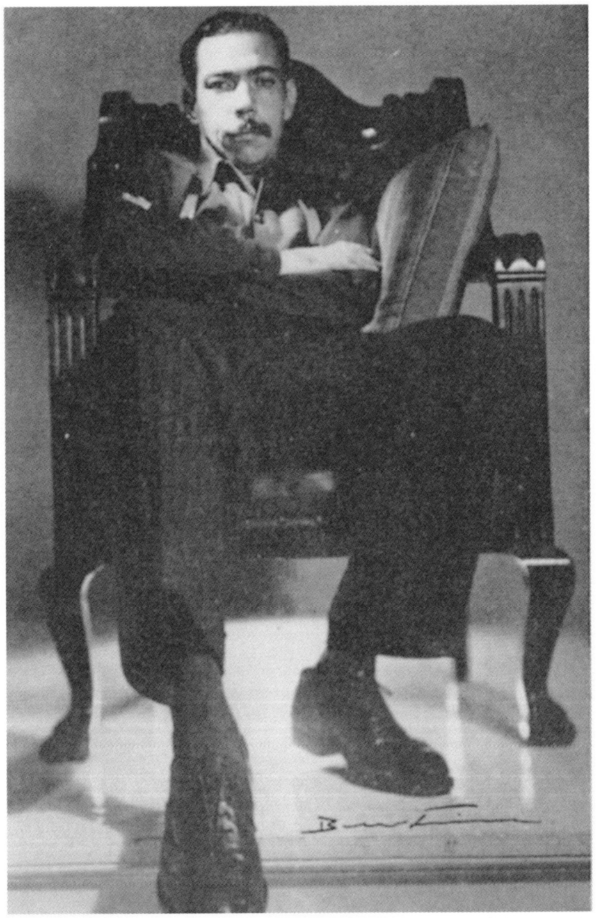

Reproduced from *Pintura Cubana de Hoy*, photograph by Berestein.

Rene Portocarrero

NOTES

1. For a study of Cuban colonial art, see Jorge Rigol, *Apuntes sobre la pintura y el grabado en Cuba* (Havana: Editorial Letras Cubanas, 1982).

2. For a study of the Minority Group, see Ana Cairo, *El Grupo Minorista y su tiempo* (Havana: Editorial Ciencias Sociales, 1978). For a study of *Revista de Avance*, see Carlos Ripoll "La Revista de Avance," *Iberoamericana* 30 (July<n>December): 261<n>82.

3. For a study of the early development of modernist Cuban painting, see Juan A. Martínez, *Cuban Art and National Identity: The Vanguardia Painters, 1927–1950* (Gainesville: University Press of Florida, 1994).

4. For a study of the Lyceum, see Luz Merino, "El Lyceum," in *Arte: Cuba Republica* (Havana: Universidad de la Habana, 1987).

5. For color reproductions of these and other paintings in the National Museum, see *The National Museum of Cuba: Painting* (Leningrad: Aurora Art Publications, 1978).

6. While there is no comprehensive study on the art of the second generation of modernist Cuban artists, there are three classical texts that touch upon it: Guy Pérez Cisneros, *Pintura y escultura en1943* (Havana: Anuario Cultural de Cuba, 1943); José Gómez Sicre, *Pintura Cubana de Hoy* (Havana: Maria Luisa Gómez Meña, 1944); and Alfred H. Barr, "Modern Cuban Painters" *Bull etin of the Museum of Modern Art* 11 (April 1944): 2–14.

7. Merino, "El Lyceum."

8. For an introduction to Los Once, see Edmundo Desnoes, "1952–1962 en la pintura cubana," in *Pintores Cubanos* (Havana: Ediciones R, 1962).

9. For a study of Sociedad Cultural Nuestro Tiempo and specifically its magazine, see Ricardo Hernández, *Revista Nuestro Tiempo* (Havana: Editorial Letras Cubanas, 1989).

10. The historiography of Cuban art was significantly expanded in the 1950s with three publications: *La Pintura y Escultura en Cuba* (Havana: Editorial Lex, 1952), a documentation of academic art in Cuba; Loló de la Torriente, *Estudio de las Artes Plásticas en Cuba* (Havana: Ucar García, 1954), a survey of Cuban art up to 1950; and Guy Pérez Cisneros, *Características de la Evolución de la Pintura en Cuba* (Havana: Dirección General de Cultura, 1959), his doctoral dissertation on Cuban colonial art.

The Photographic Tradition in Cuba

By 1840, Cuba had become an important Spanish colony with a unique location and a thriving economy. As early as November 23, 1840, merchandise stores in Havana announced that Daguerreotypes and loose plates were included in the latest shipments arriving from Europe. Newspapers throughout Havana advertised that the image of anyone could be immortalized through a Daguerreotype, which began to replace popular cameo miniatures worn in pins, buckles, and rings by Cuban ladies and gentlemen. Moreover, photography provided a less expensive product that almost every class of Cuban could treasure.

In the early 1840s, Americans and Europeans began to work in Havana as portrait photographers. During the 1860s, C. D. Fredricks, a photographer from New York, set up an influential studio in Havana and published a series of Cuban views. These photographs were mounted and numbered views of Havana and its environs. George Barnard, an employee of E. Anthony of New York, visited Cuba in 1859 and 1860, where he photographed hundreds of images for stereo viewers. Barnard then returned to the United States where he worked for the War Department during the Civil War.

Among the Cuban photographers, Don Esteban Mestre and Son created a body of work that included public and historic buildings as well as vistas and views of churches. Other important photographers of this period included José A. Soroa, López Rubio, and a host of others less well known who in 1884 formed the Association of the Friends of Photography.

Commercial demands for photographs were created from two basic areas. Salon and picturesque scenics and portraiture were prized by the rising middle class as important statements about their level of culture on the island. Postcards, announcements, and placards were in great demand by the growing numbers of shopkeepers and merchants, who fueled the expanding colonial economy increasingly based on tobacco and sugar.

Toward the end of the 1890s, the camera produced images of pure artistry comparable to the sophisticated paintings produced at the Academy of San Alejandro. Photography also became witness to historical events, including the war between Spain and the Cuban independents. At this time, countless images circulated depicting the conditions of the battlefields. Among these photographs were studies of victims of the concentration camps ordered by the Spanish General Valeriano Weyler. These powerful images and many like them became the first testimony in Cuba of a condition that was to be important in shaping the direction of photojournalism on the island. In many ways this period laid a cornerstone in the use of the photograph for propaganda later in the twentieth century. Moreover this period witnessed the development of uncommon

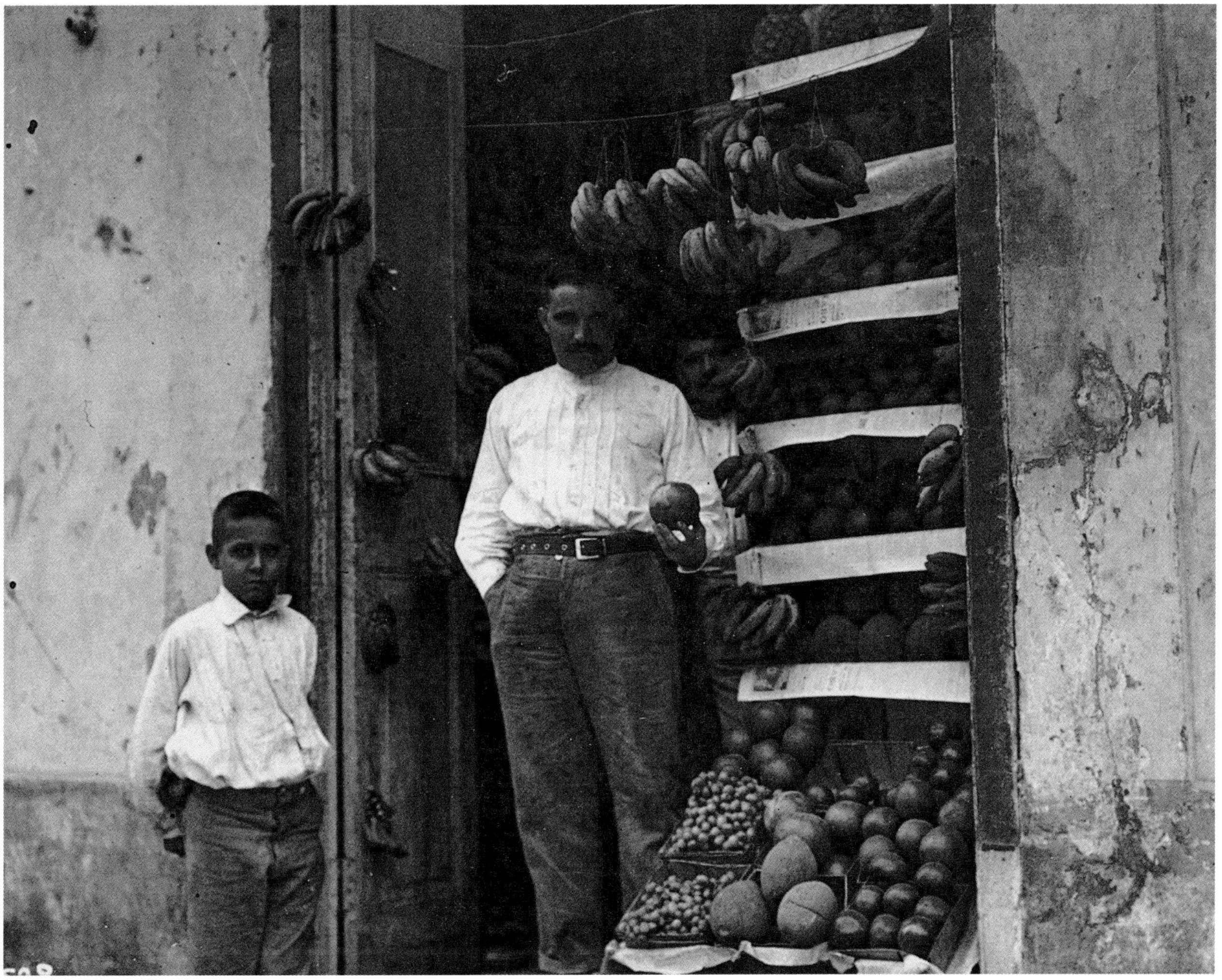

Photographer unknown, Fruit Vendor, Havana. *1900, Albumen print, 8" x 10". Gift of Ramiro Fernandez.*

technical skill and a high level of aesthetic achievement. The Cuban photography collection of the Museum of Arts and Sciences includes work by some of the acknowledged major Cuban figures noted in the chronology, as well as work by unknown Cuban nonprofessionals and North American photographers who visited the island. Taken together, these artists record historical moments, social customs, views of the island, and the many faces of Cuba's heterogeneous people. It is our hope that examples from this collection included here, while in no way comprehensive, preserve the brilliantly revealing and creative work of photographers who worked in Cuba from 1860 to 1920 and will serve as an introduction to this body of artistically and historically significant work.

Gary R. Libby

A Selected Review of Cuban Photography

1839–1921

March 28, 1839

El Diario, Havana's newspaper, published the first mention of photography in Cuba in an article translated from *La Gazette de France*, dated February 6, about J. M. Daguerre's "method of fixing images," shortly after the Daguerreotype was presented to the Academy of Science in France.

July 18, 1840

Ramis Bookstore, located on Obrapia Street, announced the sale of the book *Historic Exposition and Description of Daguerreotype Procedures*, written by J. M. Daguerre and edited by Joaquin Hisern y Molleras.

November 23, 1840

El Buen Gusto de Paris, a store at 27 Obispo Street, announced that it had received from Europe, among other things, "Daguerreotype and Daguerreotype plates." This was the earliest mention of the arrival of the Daguerreotype in Cuba.

January 3, 1841

In advertisements, George Washington Halsey announced that he was "completely qualified to do portraits of ladies and gentlemen in a room or in the large roof garden of the house at number 26, Obispo Street."

February 18, 1841

The Havana press commented on "the experiments with a drawing photogenic appliance made by Mr. Antonio Rezzónico, who has come from New York with one machine for producing miniature portraits and two for landscapes, both with the clarity of daylight." He worked at 218 Vives Street outside the walls of Havana.

June 24, 1841

R. W. Holt announced in Havana that he was able to produce portraits that were "three times as large as any previously known Daguerreotypes, and framed with golden borders. These pictures cost the same as Mr. Halsey's–one half-ounce."

July 27, 1841

The Royal Patriotic Society's printing shop announced that it was distributing the ninth edition of *Picturesque Island of Cuba,* which included photographs of the following: the Church of the Saint Christ of Havana; the Fountain of the Illustrious Havana, located in front of the Camp of Mars; "the halting place of the iron road" in the former Botanical Garden; and "the natural phenomenon in the pasture ground" of Mr. Manual Lomba (Güines). "The first two views were taken by Daguerreotype. The other two were particularly fine, having been lithographed with exquisite accuracy."

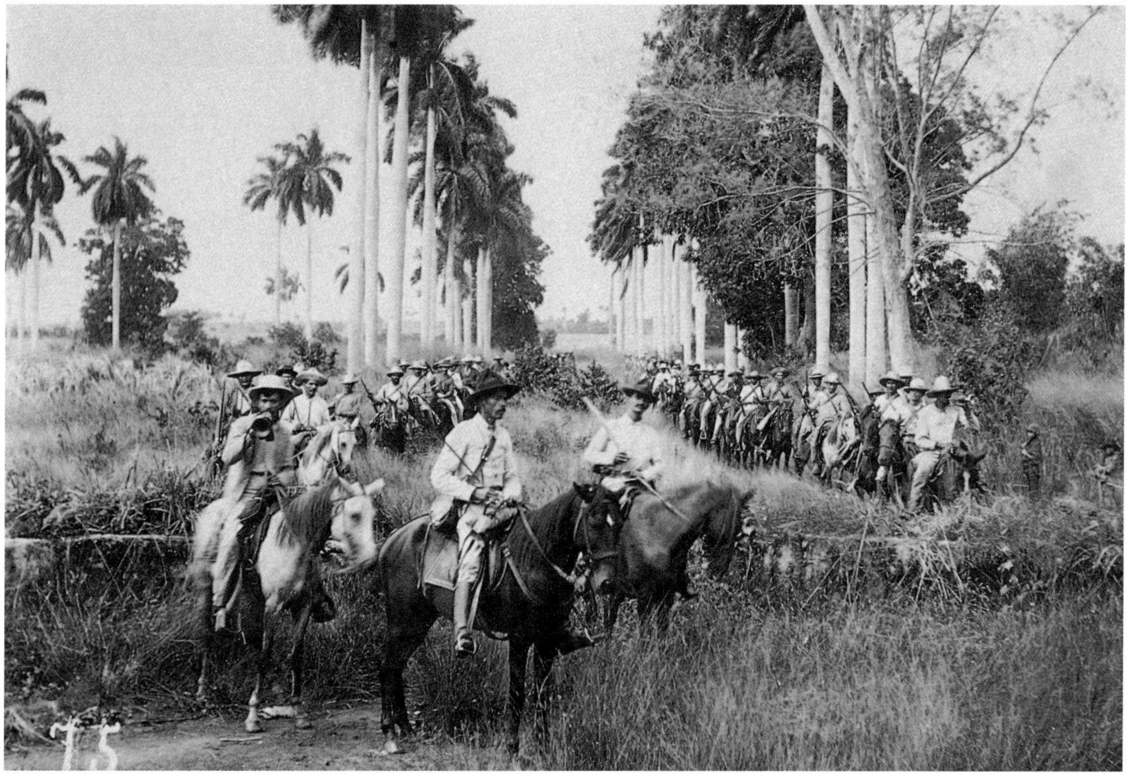

Photographer unknown, Cuban Insurgents during the War of Independence from Spain. *1885, Albumen print, 6" x 8". Gift of Ramiro Fernandez.*

October 2, 1841

On this date, the first announcement was published of Daguerre's Grand Diorama, located at 110 Obispo Street, Havana.

June 21, 1844

Esteban Arteaga, "native to this island and just arrived from Paris," advertised in the Havana newspaper *Diario de la Marina* that he could produce "the best Daguerreotype portraits under the name 'Daguerreotype with colors' at 71 Lamparilla Street . . . true likeness."

October 10, 1848

In Havana, an announcement was made by H. Custin of Berlin, who offered to solve "a problem which until now had made it almost impossible to make perfect portraits of children and family groups." This was done by applying electrogalvanism to the Daguerreotype, a technique perfected in London by Farraday, involving the application of a gold solution to fix the image.

March 6, 1851

The press announced that Juan Federico Berserling, a native of Sweden who had recently arrived in Havana, "has discovered a marvelous procedure by which he can give Daguerreotype portraits on paper and metal plates a very natural color as in the best miniatures." The photographic studio of Esteban Mestre was established at 19 O'Reilly Street, Havana.

August 17, 1852

Diario de la Marina published the first advertisement featuring the paper portraits of D. M. Payne. The portraits were prepared by a chemical procedure "that gives them an aspect as good as miniature portraits made on ivory. It can be said that they last longer than images made on metal sheets and that they can be seen perfectly under any light."

1855

Revista de la Habana published an article, "Photography Dedicated to the Photographers of La Habana," signed by J. Garcia. This article explored the possibilities of using photography in journalism.

July 3, 1857

Diario de la Habana reported that the Galeria Daguerre, 79 Obispo Street, processed portraits in all sizes, in both black and white and color. The gallery had the largest camera in Havana and sold photographs made by Parisian artists as well as stereoscopes and stereopticon photographs of France, Italy, and Switzerland on glass, paper, or metal sheets.

November 28, 1857

Photographers Fredricks and Penabert, "owners of a large successful business in the city of New York," settled at 98 Obispo Street. The Hungarian photographer Pal Rosti began to photograph scenes of Havana.

March 4, 1858

The photographic firm of Molina and Lunar, located at 44 O'Reilly Street, announced the opening of a new portrait gallery "as good as the best in Europe." Their images were known throughout the island, as well as in foreign countries, as "Molinatypes," or "miniature Daguerreotypes on crystal which are clear and brilliant with beautiful backgrounds and scenes according to the customer's taste."

May 10, 1858

Mestre's Photographic Gallery announced that it had obtained the "Royal Privilege" for its color photographs and for Mestre's "latest invention–Ambrotype portraits–which have an almost embossed appearance on backgrounds of transparent colors which enhance the beauty and softness of the portraits."

January 2, 1859

The New Gallery of Photography at 89 Obispo Street was opened by Winter, Cohner and Company, artists and photographers from Philadelphia and Washington. They specialized in the Ivorytype.

1860

In the *Directory of Arts, Commerce, and Industry of Havana*, the following photographers were listed: L. Cabrera, Juan B. Fernández and Co., O. B. Loomis and Lunar. Under "Photographic Galleries" were mentioned José M. Cotera, Esteban Mestre, La Daguerre of Carlos E. Serpa, and the Photographic Museum of José López Molina. O. B. Loomis made his Photographic Panorama of Havana.

1862

In this year, the following galleries opened: Narcisco Mestre at 19 O'Reilly Street, where his father, Esteban Mestre, was located: Lunar, Herrera and Serrano at 67 O'Reilly Street;

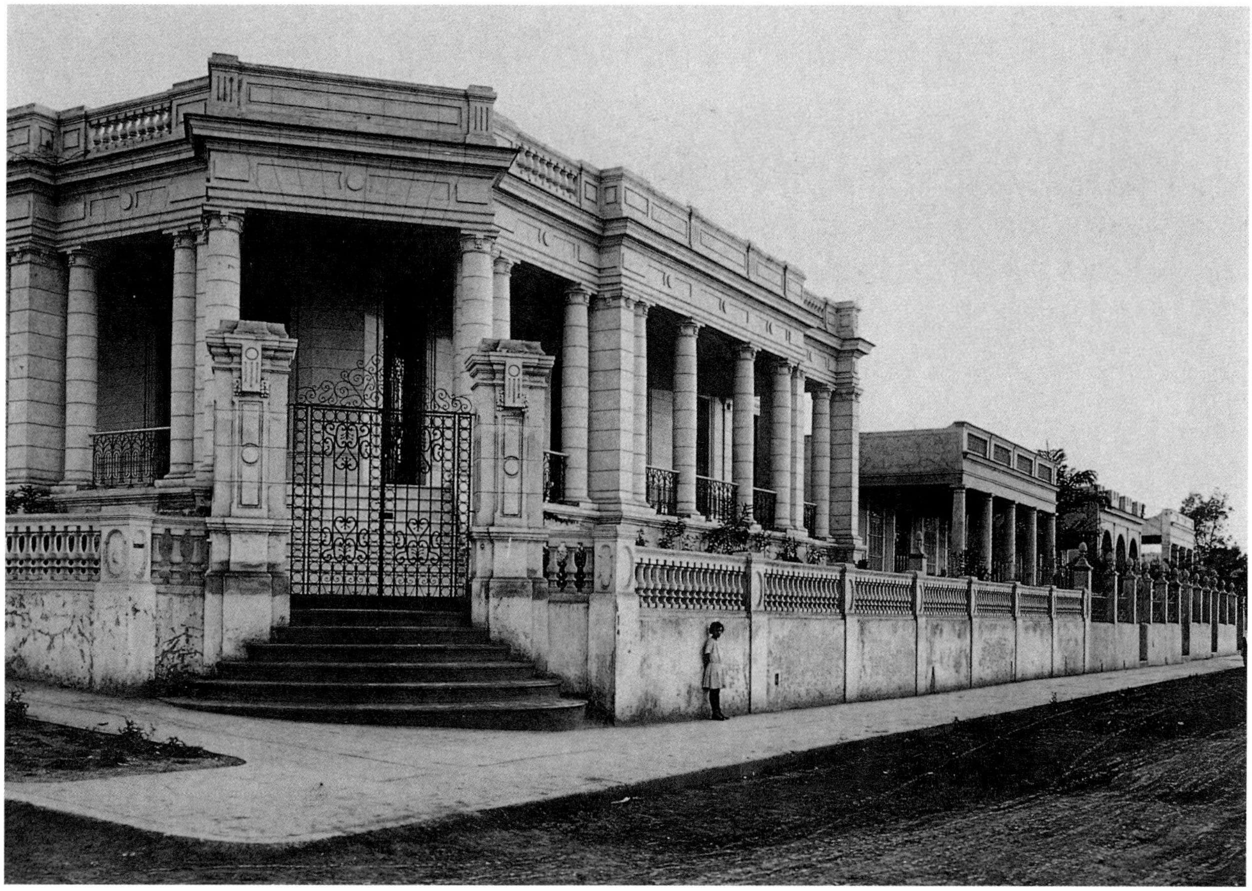

Photographer unknown, El Vedado, Havana. *1910, Silver print, 8" x 10". Gift of Ramiro Fernandez.*

Carlos D. Fredricks and Company at 108 Habana Street; and S. A. Cohner at 63 O'Reilly Street, after dissolving his brief partnership with Fredricks.

November 12, 1862

The American Gallery located at 63 O'Reilly Street advertised in *Diario de la Marina* that they could produce "night portraits" with the light of a lantern brought from Europe for that purpose.

1863

Ernesto Bavastro and Aguero photographed Santiago Bay for a series of landscapes called the "Oriental Department of the Island of Cuba," later lithographed by Emilio Lamy and C. Collet.

1865

The partnership of C. D. Fredricks and Daries was established at 108 Habana Street.

1868

Miss Domitila Garcia published the *Poetic and Photographic Album of Cuban Female Writers* dedicated to Mrs. Doña Gertrudis Gómez de Avellaneda.

1870

Using photos made by Verela and Suárez, Don Gil Gelpí and Ferro published *The Historic and Photographic Album of the Cuban War from Its Beginning until the Reign of Amadeo I.* Dedicated to the Meritorious Corps of the Army, Navy, and Volunteers of this Island.

1873

In the *General Commercial Directory of La Habana, Cuba*, published by F. Caine and Company, fifteen photographers and their galleries were registered. The most important were S. A. Cohner, Fredricks and Daries, Narciso Mestre, and Verela Suárez and Company.

1878

J. A. Suárez and Company, Photographers, was established.

1881

Alfredo Pereira Taveira started the first photographic workshop in Cuba. He phototyped the illustrations of Victor Patricio de Landaluze for the book *Types and Costumes of the Island of Cuba*, a collection of literary and graphic sketches published in Havana by Miguel de Villa.

January 1882

Published monthly by D. G. López of 1 Ena Street, Havana, the *Photographic Bulletin* was the first publication in Cuba to specialize in photography. In its first issue, the *Bulletin* summarized the general state of photography in Cuba, describing Ambrotypes, Irontypes, negatives on crystal, and photographic cards used for portraits in fashion. Other "new procedures" included the substitution of silver salts for any salt affected by light; carbon prints; enamel on crystal and porcelain; the dry procedures with collodion; and the dry gelatin plate "which constituted the last novelty and the ultimate perfection" for photographs. The principal research at the time was directed toward the production of the photogravure with natural color, as well as speeding up the photographic process with a powder or gas light so that pictures could be taken in theaters, ballrooms, and outdoors at night.

March 23, 1883

The first photogravure published in Cuba appeared in *El Museo*, a magazine in Havana. The photo of Don Nicolás Azcárate was made by Taveira.

April 16, 1883

The Association of Amateur Photographers of Havana was founded.

1884

In the *General Directory of the Island of Cuba* for the years 1884–85, twenty-seven photographers were listed. The most influential were Cohner, Fredricks, Maceo, Mestre, Suárez and Co., Casañas, Desquirón, and Ibáñez.

May 23, 1890

A photograph of the great fire of Havana, on May 17, appeared in the newspaper *La Lucha*. The snapshot was taken by the journalist Steegers.

January 1893

José Gómez de la Carrera began his brilliant career as a photographer-journalist for *El Figaro*.

1895–98

The War of Cuban Independence was documented by a large group of photographers, including Miles, Gómez de la Carerra, Gregorio Casañas, Ramón Carreras, Pérez Argení, Luis López, Desquirón, Elias Ibáñez, Mestre, Otero, and Colominas.

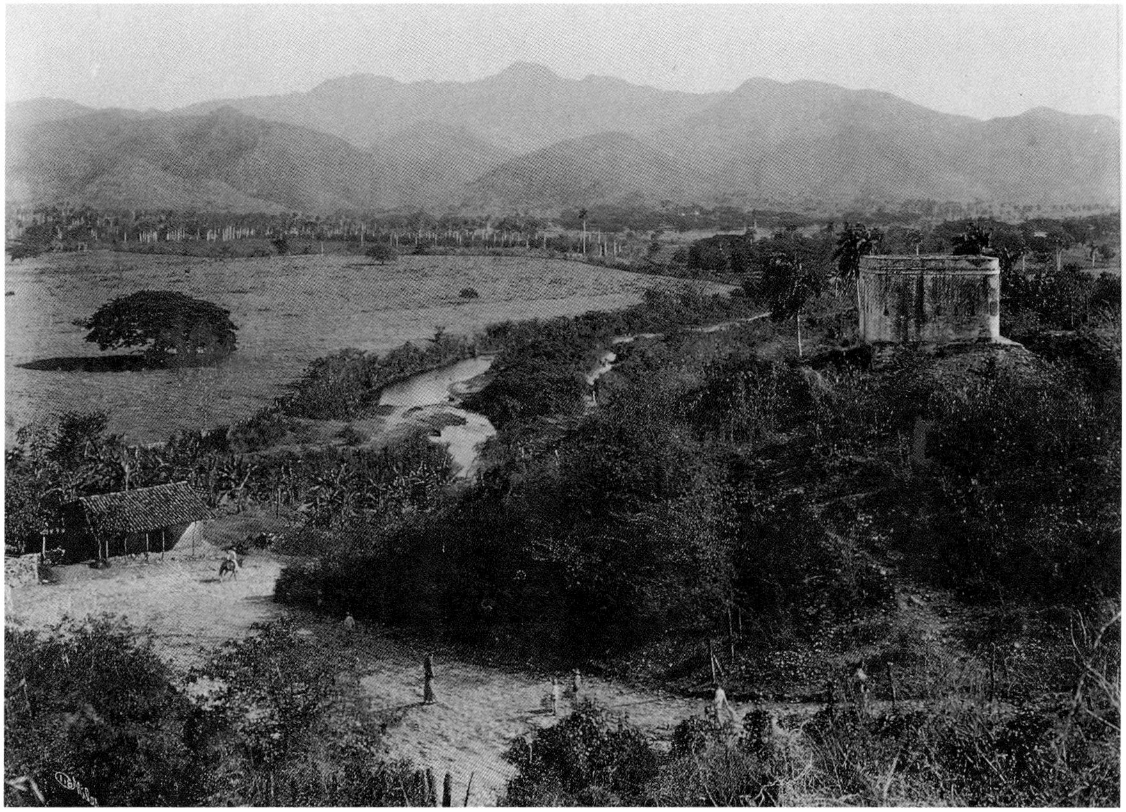

Miles, Cuban landscape with Spanish blockhouse. *1898, Albumen print, 8" x 10". Gift of Mrs. Helen Suck.*

July 28, 1899

In *La Lucha*, Count Kostia published an article on the merits of Ricardo Téstar's introduction of platinum photography in Cuba.

1901

El Mundo was founded; Adolfo Roqueñi became its first staff photographer.

1902

The *1902 Directory of Commerce, Professions, and Industry of the Island of Cuba* announced seventy galleries of photography in the country; thirty-eight were in Havana. The most prestigious galleries were those of S. A. Cohner. Téstar and Handel, and Otero and Colominas, who dissolved their partnership shortly thereafter.

May 20, 1902

At the beginning of the first "pseudorepublic," Adolfo Roqueñi, a photographer for *El Mundo*, reported that the Cuban flag replaced that of the United States. *El Figaro*, in its June 1 issue, published four of Roqueñi's pictures.

September 20, 1903

The collaboration between *El Figaro* and Gómes de la Carrera was interrupted after his article was published about President Estrada Palma leaving from Villanueva Station on a trip through the country. After this date, Gómez de la Carrera worked only sporadically for *El Figaro*.

1904

Rafael Blanco Santa Coloma was named special photographer for *El Figaro*. As a result of his intensive work for this publication, Coloma became the most important photojournalist of the early years of the republic. Until his death, he also worked for *Diario de la Marina* and *Heraldo de Cuba*.

August 24, 1906

In the newspaper *La Discusión*, Federico Gilbert Garcia published his well-known photograph of the assassinated General Quintin Banderas. Gilbert Garcia was an important photojournalist in the early years of the Cuban republic. He set up the first photography and photo engraving workshops for the newspapers, and he taught many graphic journalists of the Cuban press.

May 17, 1908

Bohemia, a magazine of great importance in the development of Cuban photojournalism, was first published.

August 22, 1909

El Figaro published "The Soldiers of Photography," signed by "the Chroniqueur." The goal of this article was to characterize the first Cuban photojournalists, such as Gómez de la Carrera, Luis and Sergio Camino, Federico Gilbert, Julio Lagomasino, Rafael Blanco Santa Coloma, Ricardo Pijuán, Javier Salas, and José López y López.

January 1916

The magazine *Social* began publication. During its early years, *Social* listed the following journalists: Joaquín Blez, José López y López, Karl Handel, Colominas, Goodknows, A. Martínez, Jaime Gispert (a Spaniard living in Cuba), Manuel Villas, and Ricardo Pijuán ("the bride's photographer"). The American Photo, a gallery that opened immediately after the republic was established, also collaborated with this magazine.

1917

The first aerial photographs of Cuba were taken by Adolfo Roqueñi.

1919

Carteles was founded. Enrique Figarola (Kiko) collaborated with this magazine during its early years. *Carteles* changed its format in May 1924, when graphics became its focus and its most powerful journalistic tool. Federico Gilbert Garcia, with a Graflex camera, took the first snapshot of a jai alai game in Almendares Park.

1921

The flash bulb was introduced in Cuba.

This chronology was selected and edited from information contained in a catalogue of a *Retrospective Exhibition of Photography in Cuba* at the National Museum of Fine Art, Havana, 1983.

Gary R. Libby

Opposite page:
Photographer unknown, *Havana, City Scene,*
ca. 1908, Silver print, 10" x 8",
from the collection of Ramiro Fernandez.

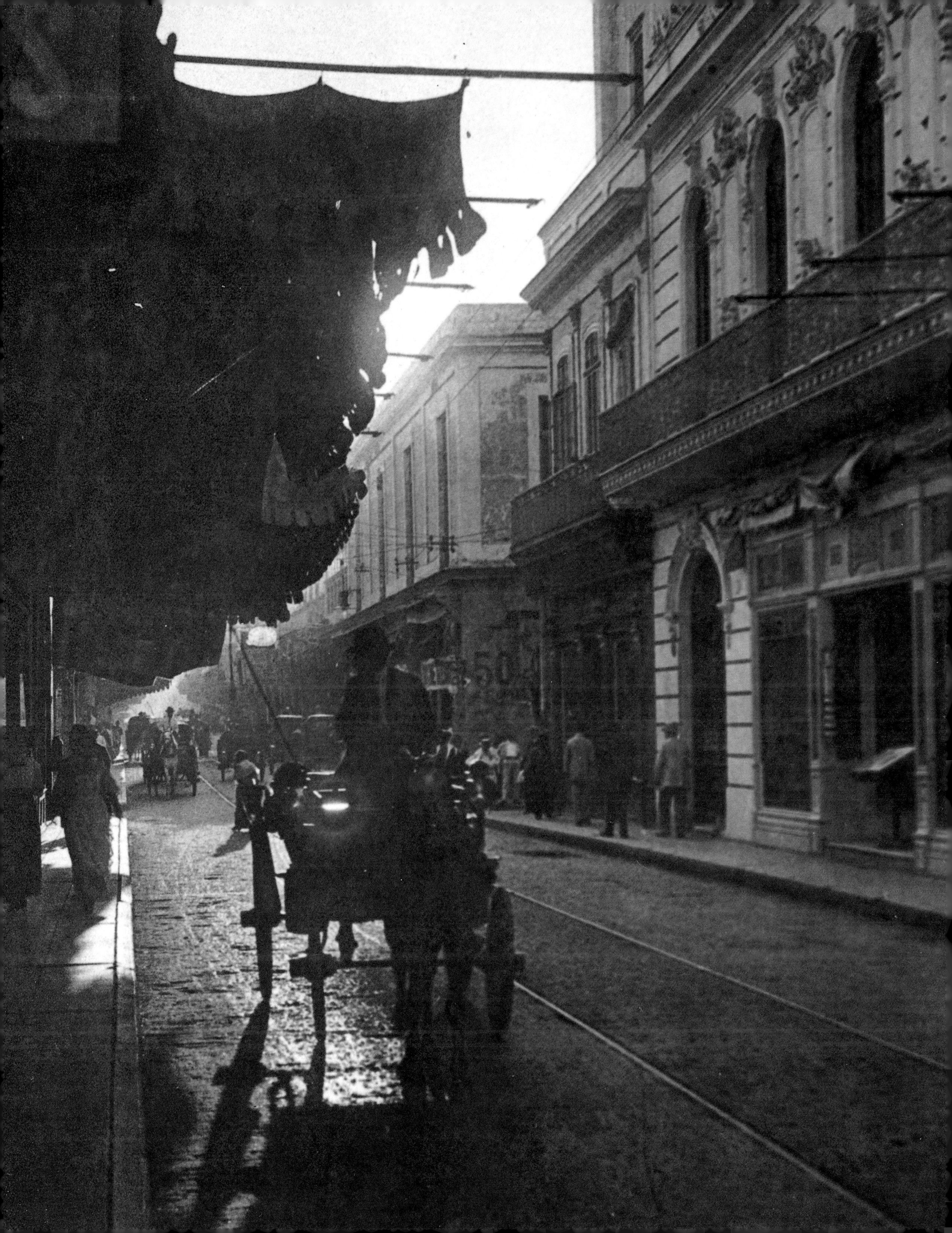

A Note on the Cuban Foundation Collection

A Florida and National Treasure

The Cuban Foundation Collection of the Museum of Arts and Sciences has enjoyed an exciting history since the revolution of 1959 in Cuba. Before that event, President Fulgencio Batista and his second wife, Marta, gave paintings, prints, and folk art that reflected Cuban history and culture to a newly established foundation, they had created in the United States. The Batistas also personally collected Spanish and Italian art, but it was this collection that was to establish the basis for the present Cuban Foundation Collection of the Museum of Arts and Sciences.

After 1959, when the Batistas established residency in Portugal and finally in Spain, the Foundation Collection of Cuban academic, modernist, and folk art, gifted to the city of Daytona Beach in 1957, resided in a house museum given and endowed by the Batistas and designed to keep Cuban history alive as Castro tightened his grip on the island and its rich Hispanic culture. The core collection contained twenty-seven major paintings, forty-five ceramics and items of folk culture, models of Cuban architecture and industry, and personal items including furniture once owned by President and Mrs. Batista. Soon after, the city of Daytona Beach invited the Museum of Arts and Sciences to occupy the Cuban Museum and operate it in the public trust. In 1970, final plans for a larger modern facility for the Museum of Arts and Sciences were finalized, and the Batista family allowed for the sale of the original riverfront property and the transfer and movement of the collection to a new contemporary home as a permanent collection at the Museum of Arts and Sciences, on the mainland of Daytona Beach located in a ninety-acre park preserve. The Museum of Arts and Sciences and the Cuban Foundation care for the collection in perpetuity.

The original collection and gifts were reinstalled in a renovated permanent home at the Museum in 1980, after a tour of the state of Florida with venues at the Ringling Museum of Art, Sarasota, the Tampa Museum of Art, and the new State of Florida Legislative Building in Tallahassee. The Cuban Foundation Museum was again renovated in 1996 when the collection was reinstalled including recent gifts.

Since its inception, the Cuban Foundation Collection has grown through generous gifts from many donors including Marshall Stewart, who donated the rare and important Eduardo Laplante lithographs illustrated here. Elias Drymonis was the generous donor of two highly significant still lifes by J. Gil Garcia. The late Mary Humphrey Cameron donated Cuban jewelry and a very early Madonna from the first cathedral in Havana, while the late Anderson C. Bouchelle gifted Cuban paintings, colonial silver, and decorative arts. Marc and Joanne Davidson have given important maps and decorative arts to the collection. Mr. and Mrs. Allen Dine have gifted colonial furniture as has John Georgoudiou. The late Kenneth Worcester Dow and his late wife, Mary, donated important pieces of colonial furniture and fine art to the collection. Ramiro Fernandez, noted New York photography collector, and Winter Park, Florida, resident Helen Suck gifted both salon and picturesque photographs to the museum and its growing Cuban Foundation Collection of fine and folk art.

Since the original donation, the number of items in the collection has more than tripled. The collection has also broadened through the introduction of New World Spanish Colonial objects including those from Cuba.

Today, the collection is housed in a 2,500-square-foot gallery at the Museum of Arts and Sciences where objects in the collection are rotated for exhibition as new items arrive through gifts, donations, and purchases. A Florida and national treasure, the collection also continues to function as a major source of original objects available for loan to museums and institutions worldwide who are interested in the rich artistic culture of Cuba.

Gary R. Libby

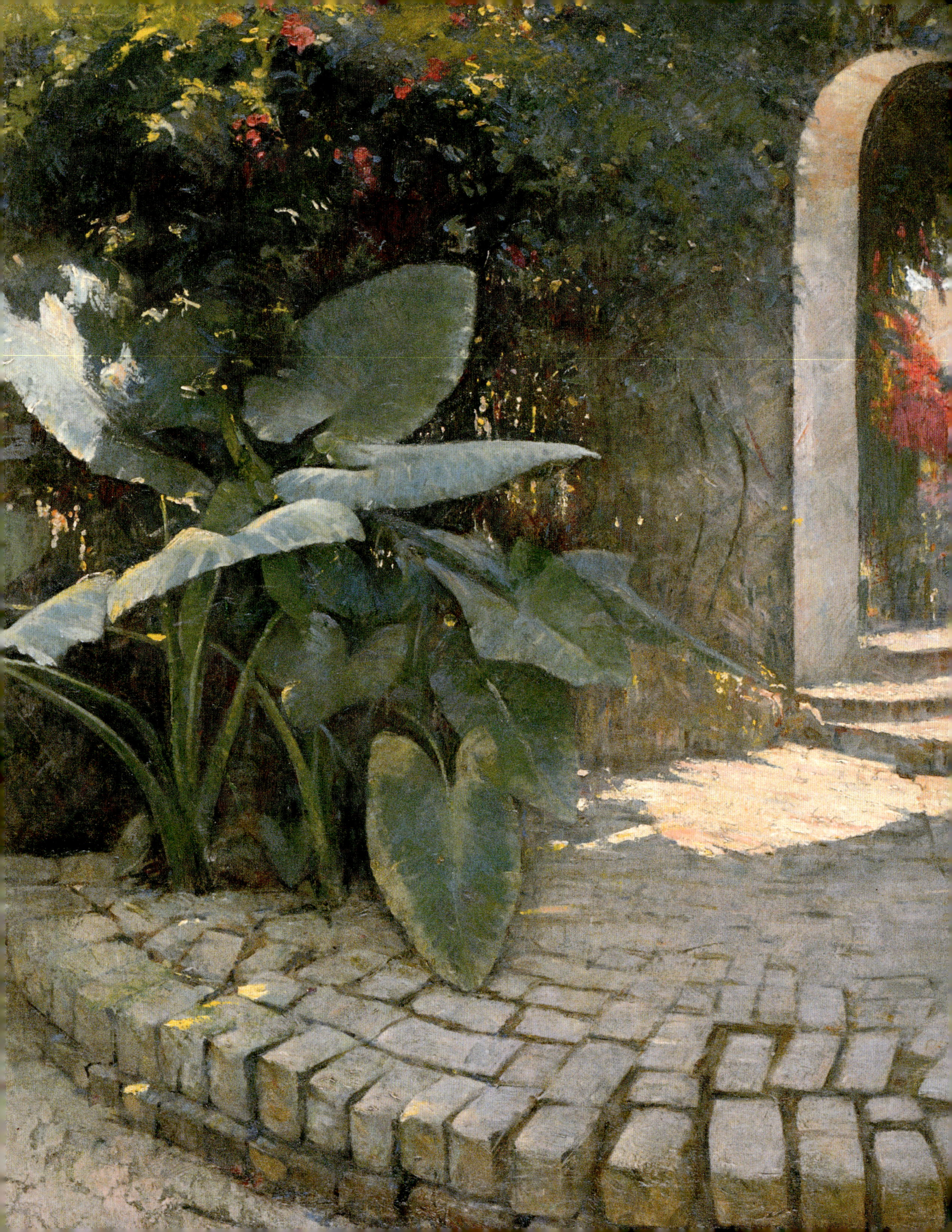

THE CATALOGUE

Opposite page: Detail,
Corner in a Cuban Garden, Emilio Rivero Merlin.

Latino Paintings

Late Eighteenth Century–Unknown Artist

This series of four paintings in the collection of the Museum of Arts and Sciences in Daytona Beach is among the most important extant visual records defining the origin and nature of popular racial culture in the Spanish New World. As artistic statements, they record four family portraits resplendent with costumes and accoutrements in an indefinite shallow outdoor space. As sociological statements, they record many of the rich and diverse basic racial components of Latino culture in colonial New World Spain, including Cuba, where Spanish, African, and Indian inhabitants produced a people and a culture of great heterogeneity and vitality.

The first of the four paintings represents

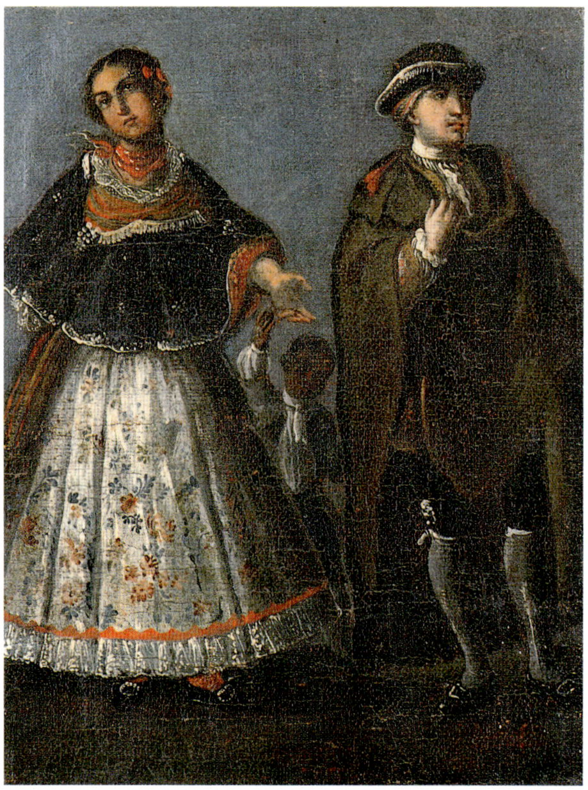

Painting #1
Late eighteenth century, Oil on canvas, 13" x 10"
Gift of Anderson C. Bouchelle

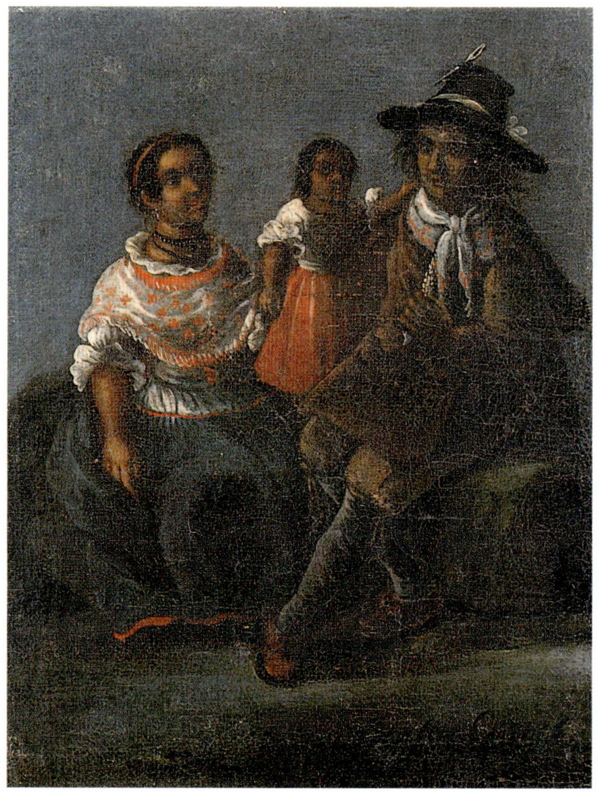

Painting #2
Late eighteenth century, Oil on canvas, 13" x 10"
Gift of Anderson C. Bouchelle

a Spanish gentleman with his Spanish-Indian wife and son. The second canvas illustrates an Indian-African man and his Indian wife and child. The third canvas captures a gentleman of Spanish, Indian, and African racial background with his Spanish wife and daughter. The fourth canvas illustrates a man of Spanish-Indian background with his African wife and son. In each canvas, skin color, facial features, and costume help identify the origins of the subjects and draw attention to the multicultural population and cross-cultural environment created when cultures literally cross-fertilize each other in New World Spain, including Cuba. G.R.L.

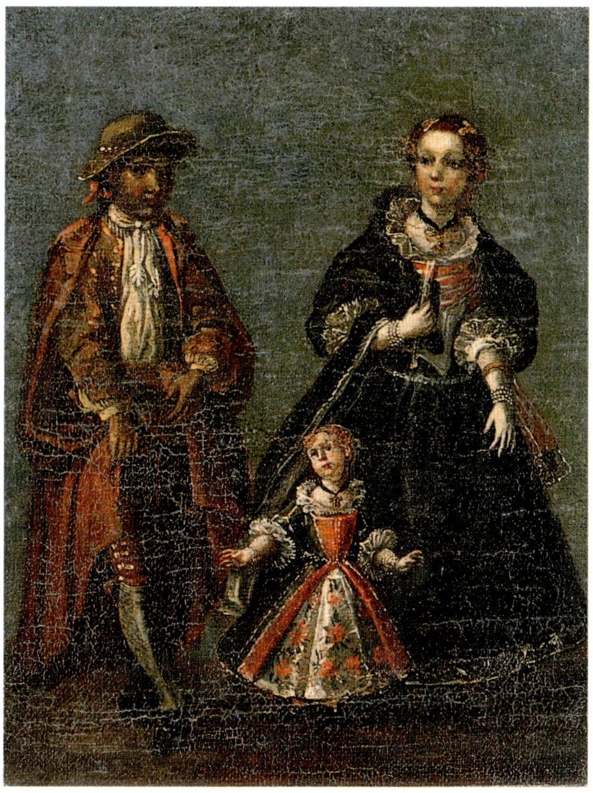

Painting #3

Late eighteenth century, Oil on canvas, 13" x 10"

Gift of Anderson C. Bouchelle

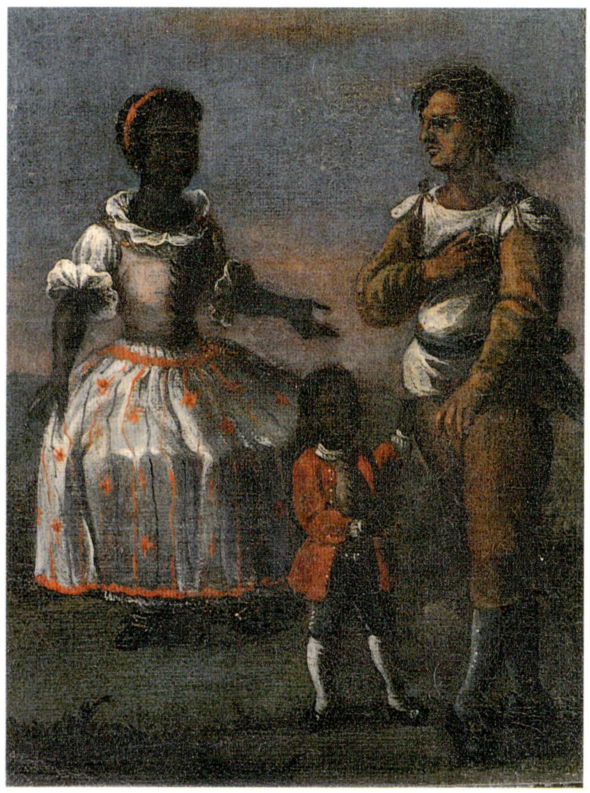

Painting #4

Late eighteenth century, Oil on canvas, 13" x 10"

Gift of Anderson C. Bouchelle

José Nicolás de la Escalera

1734–1804

Known as the first great painter to be recorded in Cuba, de la Escalera was born in 1734. While his birthplace is still unknown, most scholars agree that he was most certainly Cuban and probably of Mestizo-Latino origin. He died in Havana in 1804. His religious decorations and painting represent the restrained and elegant Counter-Reformation Jesuit Baroque style, as it was expressed in Cuba in the second half of the eighteenth century. This style of art attempted to capture the attention of the faithful and to win wayward Protestants back to the Catholic faith by creating works of art filled with emotional drama and spiritual majesty. It shows close affinity to polychromed religious wood carvings of the period, many of which were imported from Spain and may have served as models for paintings of saints and other religious subjects by de la Escalera.

The *Coronation of the Virgin by the Trinity* is a large and impressive example of de la Escalera's mature vision. Here the Madonna, clothed in white and blue, levitates majestically toward a red-robed Jesus and God the Father, who together hold a golden crown and officiate at Mary's impending coronation. Overhead, the Holy Spirit represented by a glowing white dove completes the Trinity as the Virgin ascends to her elevated position as Queen of Heaven. Typical of the Baroque spirit, a large group of winged cherubs accompany the three principal figures. These cherubs are a consistent motif in Cuban colonial religious and decorative art. The overall double inverted triangular design of the composition and primary color harmonies of red, yellow, and blue all accentuate the restrained drama of this important celestial event in a shallow space, made modestly dramatic by a restrained cloudy chiaroscuro and a delicate, somewhat naive modeling of the figures.

The *Coronation of the Virgin by the Trinity* is a prime example of the European-inspired religious art of New Spain as it was expressed in Cuba.

G.R.L.

Bibliography:
José Gómez Sicre. *Pintura Cubana de Hoy.* Havana: Maria Luisa Gómez Mena, 1944.

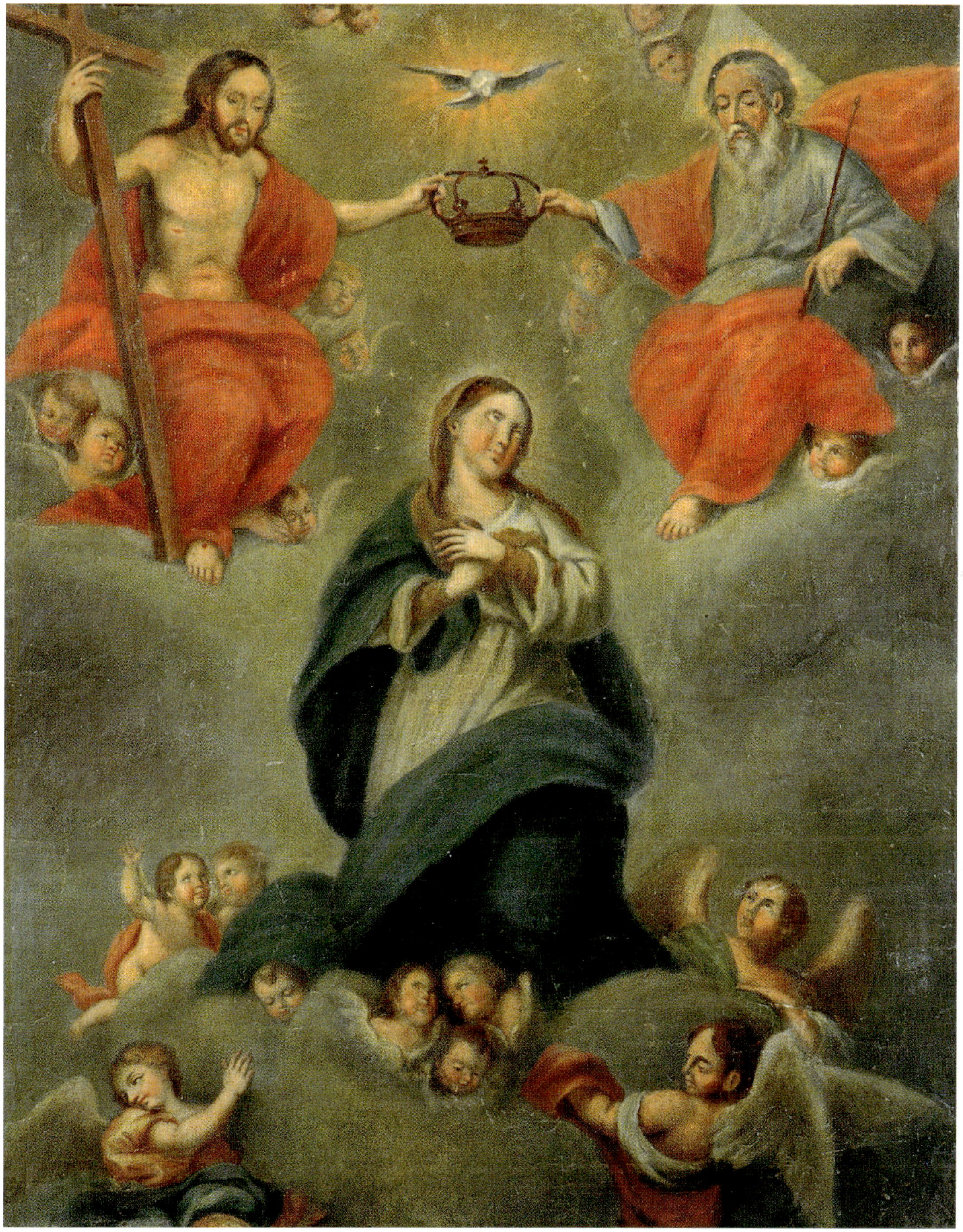

José Nicolás de la Escalera
CORONATION OF THE VIRGIN BY THE TRINITY
Late eighteenth century, Oil on board, 34" x 28"
Gift of the Cuban Foundation

Vicente Escobar

1757–1854

One of the most important portrait painters of the colonial period, Vicente Escobar was born in the environs of Havana in 1757. He died there in 1854. He was probably a "free man of color." Escobar is the first link between the formal portrait tradition of late seventeenth-century Spain and its expression in New World Cuba during the eighteenth and nineteenth centuries. He is principally known for a series of family portraits of the developing Cuban aristocracy. In his *Portrait of Don Tomas Mateo Cervantes,* Escobar captures the Cuban civic and cultural leader in realistic detail in the manner of Francisco Goya (1746–1828) yet undercut by a consistent naiveté typical of Escobar's best work.

Escobar presents Cervantes in three-quarter view dressed in his official deep blue tunic with gold braid and buttons and wearing a court or formal sword. Cervantes wears an elaborate lace cravat and cuffs, which demonstrate Escobar's skill at accurate observation and realistic detail. The white lace furthermore contrasts with the velvet texture and mass of the deep blue coat. Cervantes is captured in middle age with a youthful, inquisitive, and self-assured formality. Tucked neatly in the upper left corner of the canvas is the Cervantes coat of arms. With the bold script running along the bottom of the canvas, which reads, "Don Tomas Mateo Cervantes, Attorney General of the City, and in particular, the Monastery of Santa Clara; Acting General Administrator and Founding Member of The House of Charity," Cervantes is clearly identified as a member of the Cuban nobility and a fitting subject for this elegant portrait.

G.R.L.

Bibliography:
José Gómez Sicre. *Pintura Cubana de Hoy.* Havana: Maria Luisa Gómez Mena, 1944.

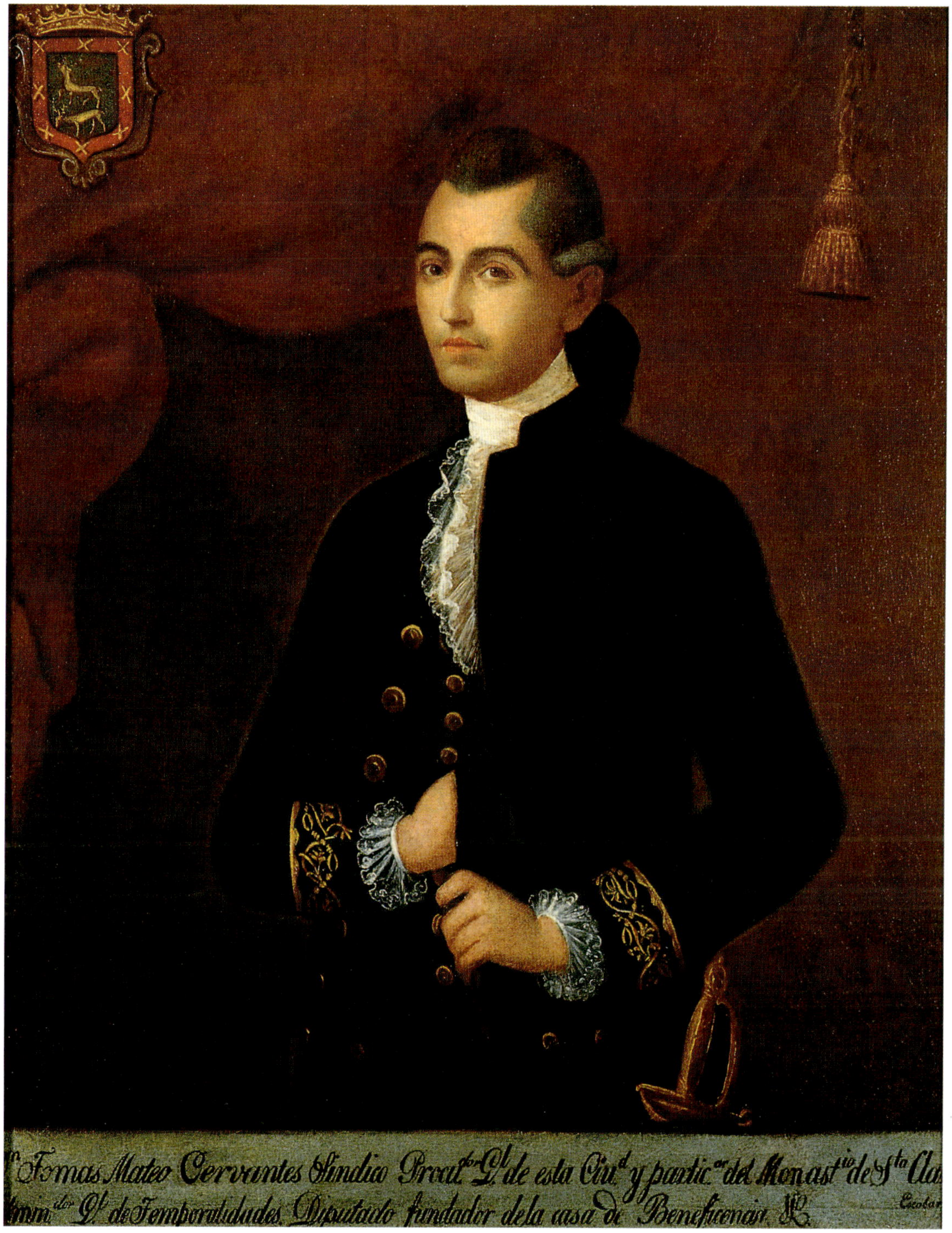

Vicente Escobar

Portrait of Don Tomas Mateo Cervantes

Ca. 1800, Oil on canvas, 60" x 39"

Gift of the Cuban Foundation

Esteban Chartrand

1840–1884

Little is known about the early life of Esteban Chartrand. He was born in Cuba in 1840 and was probably educated in Havana. His paintings clearly show the rigorous discipline of an academic background rooted in the traditional skills of accurate drawing, local color, a sophisticated knowledge and use of chiaroscuro, aerial and linear perspective, and a tendency toward the sentimental and romantic in his selection and treatment of subject matter. Chartrand is known to have first traveled to the United States sometime before 1865. Paintings with a Key West, Florida, location and paintings incorporating Charleston, South Carolina, landmarks are extant. His name appears intermittently in exhibition records along the Eastern Seaboard including Savannah, Charleston, Baltimore, and New York. Chartrand returned to Havana after contracting a respiratory ailment, probably tuberculosis, sometime before 1880. He died in Hoboken, New Jersey, in 1884 at the age of sixty.

The oil on canvas *Witches' Hut* of 1879 is an important example from Chartrand's most important period. Painted in a carefully rendered and accurate manner, Chartrand captures a mounted male rider in typical white peasant folk outfit, straw hat, and red kerchief, talking to an elderly Afro-Cuban bandana-clad woman, on foot, holding a cane for support and accompanied by her small dog. In front of her hut is a cooking fire that enlivens the center right of the composition. With the rider is a foal who stands to the left of the mare ridden by the mounted Cuban. Chartrand neatly divides the painting into foreground and background by painting an accurate rough stone wall and wooden gate directly behind the subjects. Behind the wall is a field of emblematic banana trees and a more distant landscape of symbolic palms. Light is fading, and the sky is filled with the golden glow of a sunset that frames the mysterious rising crescent moon. To the right of the hut are four gnarled pine trees filled with nesting birds including roosters, doves, and owls, all avatars of Santeria, the Afro-Cuban religion that is the implied context of this painting and an important element of Cuban folk culture. Chartrand places the Cuban man, in white, armed with a machete, physically above the Afro-Cuban woman who has emerged from the dark indefinite interior of her hut, which is the home of her powers as a Santeria priestess and fortune-teller. While we do not know the nature of the conversation, Chartrand has captured the essence of this human interaction in this private moment so important to an understanding of the multicultural richness of Cuban civilization. G.R.L.

Bibliography:
José Gómez Sicre. *Pintura Cubana de Hoy* Havana: Maria Luisa Gómez Mena, 1944.

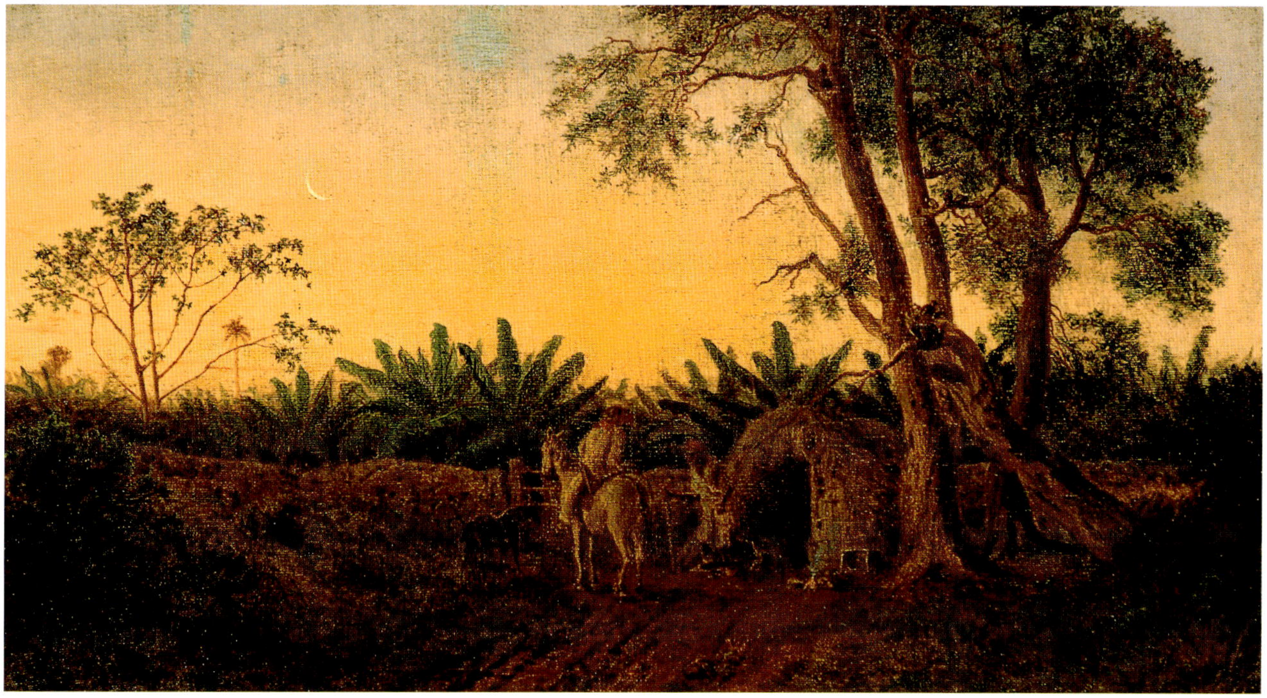

Esteban Chartrand

WITCHES' HUT

1879, Oil on canvas, 18" x 29"

Gift of the Cuban Foundation

Miguel Melero

1836–1907

Born in Havana in 1836, Miguel Melero Rodriguez studied painting and drawing in schools there before entering the Academy of San Alejandro. At the age of twenty he won his first serious prize for a portrait painting and a portrait sculpture in the annual competition at El Liceo. In 1858, he again won a gold medal for a portrait and was appointed a faculty member in fine arts at El Liceo. Melero then studied at schools in Spain, Italy, and France. He returned to Cuba and in 1878 became the director of the Academy of San Alejandro, following the charismatic and talented Francisco Cisneros. Melero excelled in historical subjects, religious subjects, and portraits painted in the grand manner of late nineteenth-century academic realism. He also continued to produce sculpture. His monumental work can be seen throughout Cuba, including his Christopher Columbus at Colón.

Melero was well received throughout his career. He served as president of the Sociedad Económica, honorary member of the Academy of Arts and Letters, Knight of the Order of Isabella the Catholic, and professor at the El Salvador School. He died in Havana in 1907.

In *Portrait of Aurelio, Son of the Artist,* completed in 1906, the year before he died, Miguel Melero presents his son, dressed in a dark formal jacket, white shirt, and a red and black striped cravat accented by a gold stickpin in the shape of an elaborate dagger. The sitter is in near profile facing right and probably posing in his father's dark studio, suggested by three unframed canvases that serve as markers for the foreground, midground, and background of the elegant and painterly portrait. The sitter, Aurelio, is middle-aged. He sports a fashionable beard and moustache in the French style. The painting is lit from the left creating a bold chiaroscuro that highlights the architecture of his face. Melero's brushstroke on the portrait is highly refined and nearly invisible. Other areas of the canvas illustrate the growing influence of a dark impressionism of rich browns and lush greens in the Spanish style, popular in Cuba at the end of the nineteenth century. G.R.L.

Bibliography:
Painting and Sculpture in Cuba. Havana: Edition of Homage,1952. Pgs. 52–53.

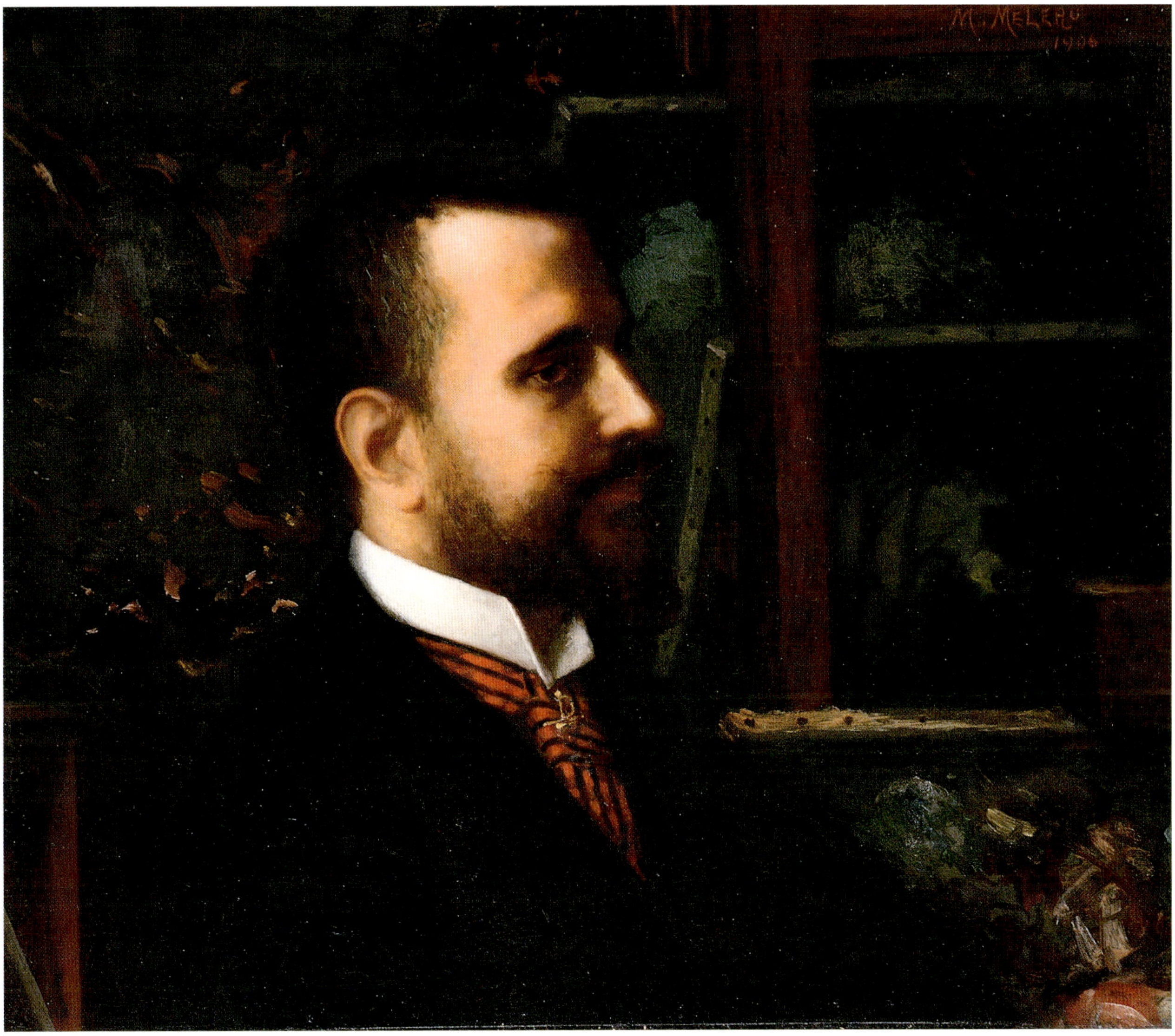

Miguel Melero

Portrait of Aurelio, Son of the Artist

1906, Oil on canvas, 21" x 25"

Gift of the Cuban Foundation

Miguel Arias

1841–1915

Miguel Arias Bordou was born in Léon, Spain. He is generally considered one of the fathers of the Cuban landscape school where the scene not only records "place" but also illustrates elements of Cuban life and culture. Other than his founding membership in the Cuban National Academy and his early work as a set designer with Antonio Rodriguez Morey in Havana, little is known about Arias's early life and training, although his mature work clearly shows the influence of the European academic tradition.

In his *Cuban Landscape* of ca. 1875, Arias unites a topographical view of a distant sugar plantation with a scene of rural agricultural life. In the foreground a farmer, dressed in a typical white outfit and straw hat, waters a horse in a clear stream painted in the high-keyed cerulean blue typical of Arias's colorist treatment of water.

In the background of this impressive landscape are the buildings of an *ingenio,* or sugar plantation and mill. Such plantations helped transform Cuba into one of the richest agricultural forces in the Caribbean region. Similar in many ways to earlier lithographs of the great sugar plantations made by Eduardo Laplante and known as *Los Ingenios de Cuba*, Arias gives us a single stacked mill used to crush and then boil down the sugar extract, two stone buildings with flat roofs, other related support structures, and a frame vernacular bungalow with large veranda where a man and woman stroll near a saddled horse. The sky is large with billowy soft clouds and a clear, consistent blue-white light. Royal palms and native vegetation dominate the expansive landscape in this arcadian statement about the synthesis of Cuban rural life, industry, and culture. G.R.L.

Bibliography:
For a bilingual biography with a photograph of the artist, see *Great Masters of Cuban Art: The Ramos Collection.* Daytona Beach, Florida, 2009. Pg. 260.

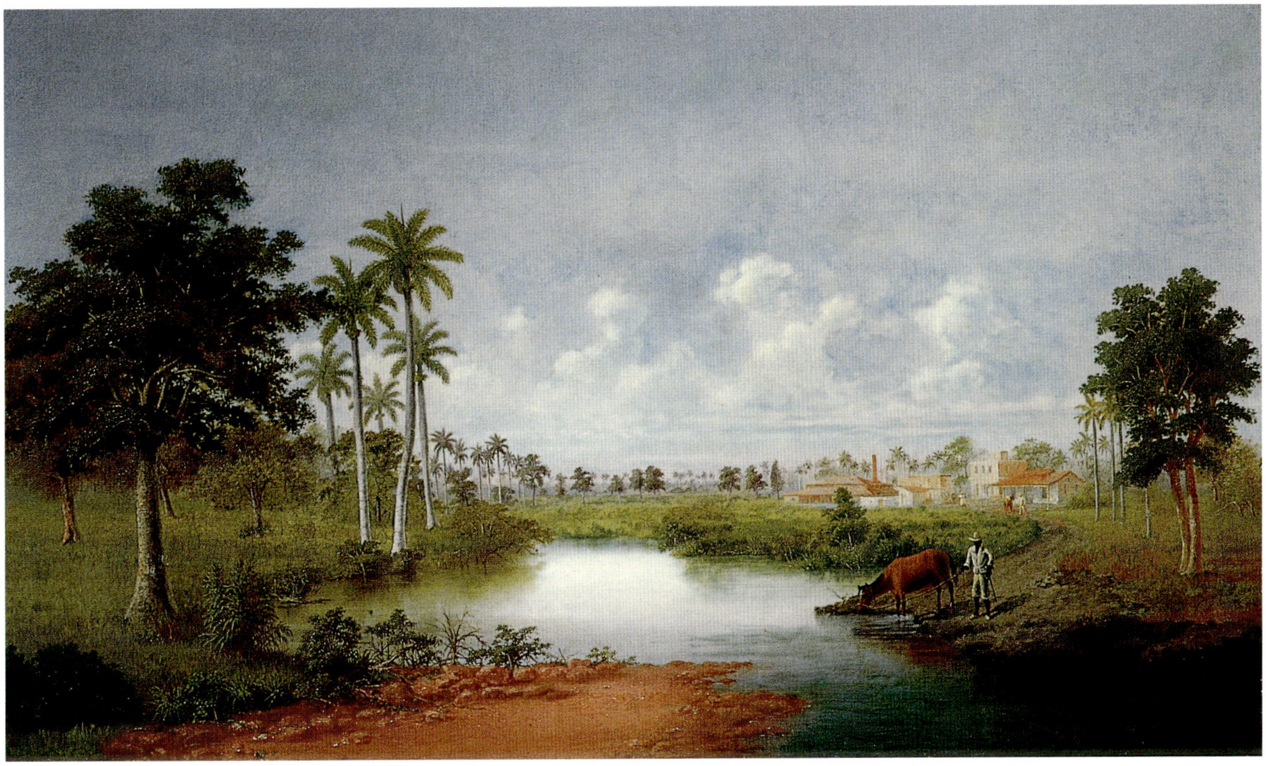

Miguel Arias

CUBAN LANDSCAPE

Ca. 1875, Oil on canvas, 23" x 41"

Gift of the Cuban Foundation

Leopoldo Romañach

1862–1951

Born in the village of Sierra Morena in Las Villas province on October 7, 1862, Leopoldo Romañach y Guillen was the son of a Catalonian father and Cuban mother.

When his mother died in 1867, Romañach was sent to the home of his uncle in Cabo Creus, Spain, in Gerona province, where he completed his early education. He then studied in Barcelona before returning to Cuba in 1877, where he worked for his father as a clerk in Vega de Palma, Camajuani. Soon Romañach was sent to New York for six months to perfect his knowledge of English.

During his early studies in Barcelona, he was influenced by work of the important Catalonian painter Mariano Fortuny. While in New York, Romañach studied the old masters in the Metropolitan Museum of Art.

In 1885, after a brief stay in Caibarien, Cuba, he returned to Havana where he enrolled in the Academy of San Alejandro for a year. He returned to Caibarien to paint. In 1889, with the support of Cuban aristocrat Francisco Ducassi and the journalist known as Bácaro, Romañach won a five-year scholarship from the government of Santa Clara to study in Rome. There Romañach studied with Spanish and Italian academicians including Filippo Prosperi, director of the Institutes of Fine Arts in Rome.

In 1895, when the Cuban War of Independence started, Romañach's scholarship was suspended and he left Rome for New York. He opened a studio and joined a group of republican expatriates including José Marti, Raimundo Cabrera, and Gonzalo de Quesada. After the revolution, Romañach returned to Havana and accepted the professorship of the study of color in 1900 at San Alejandro, after first politely declining the directorship. He served as professor at the Academy for fifty years and, together with Armando G. Menocal, prepared generations of Cubans for careers in the fine arts.

Romañach received strong, positive critical reactions to his early and mature work both inside and outside of Cuba, including a Bronze Medal in the Universal Exposition, Paris, 1900; a Gold Medal in the St. Louis Exposition of 1904; a Silver Medal in the Buffalo, New York, Exposition of 1904; and a Gold Medal in the Exposition of Charleston, South Carolina, in 1905. He was awarded the Grand Cross of the Cuban National Order of Merit. In 1950 he was appointed professor emeritus and honorary director of the Academy of San Alejandro. Romañach died in Havana on September 10, 1951.

On the Way to Mass is a celebrated work from Romañach's most important period. It portrays a mature Cuban lady dressed in a traditional yet somewhat daring and voluminous black dress and mantilla. Her left hand gently touches her left breast while her right hand holds a prayer book and rosary, suggesting the dual nature, both sensual and spiritual, of her world. Romañach does not dwell on minute

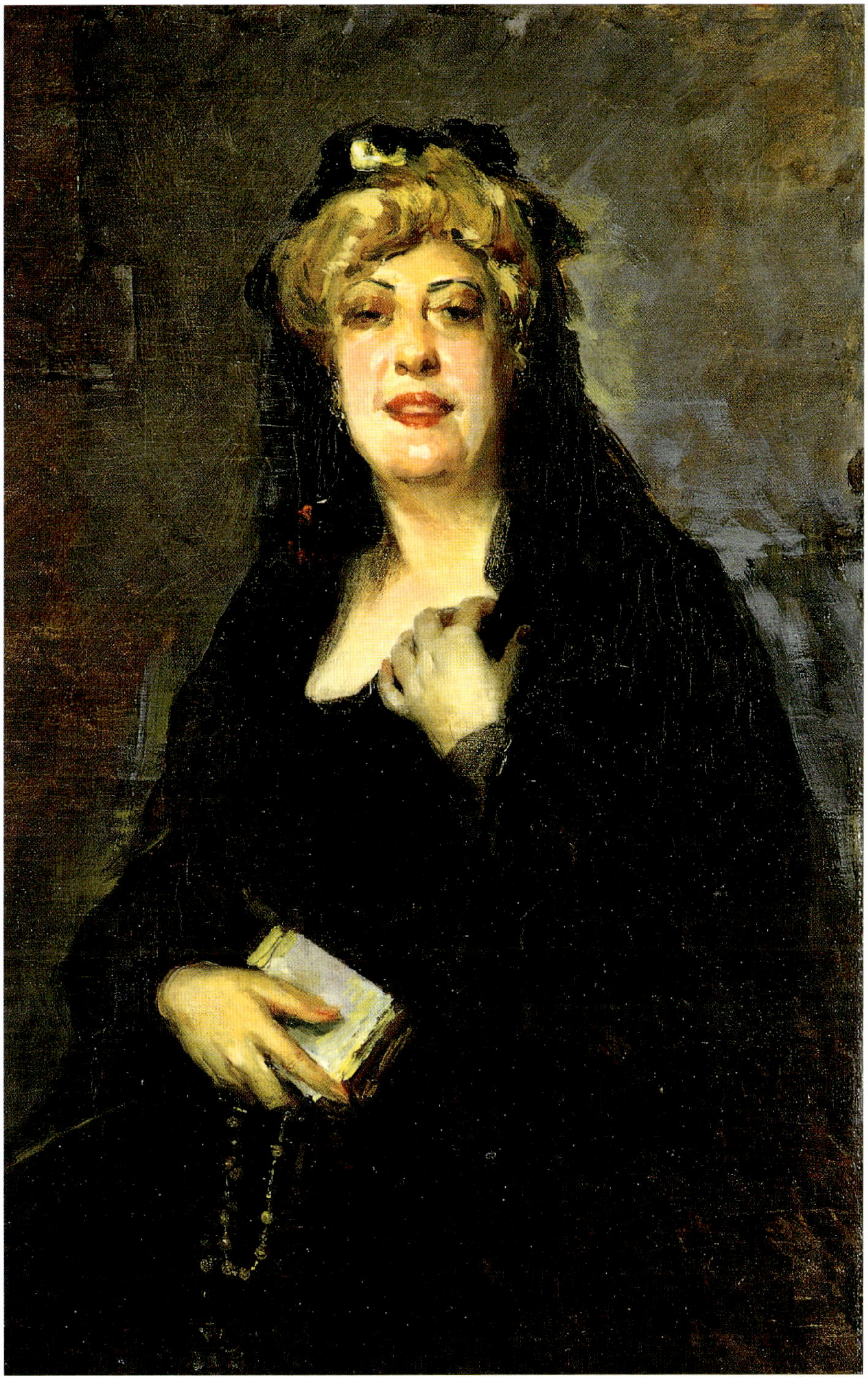

Leopoldo Romañach

ON THE WAY TO MASS

Ca. 1930, Oil on canvas, 59" x 31"

Gift of the Cuban Foundation

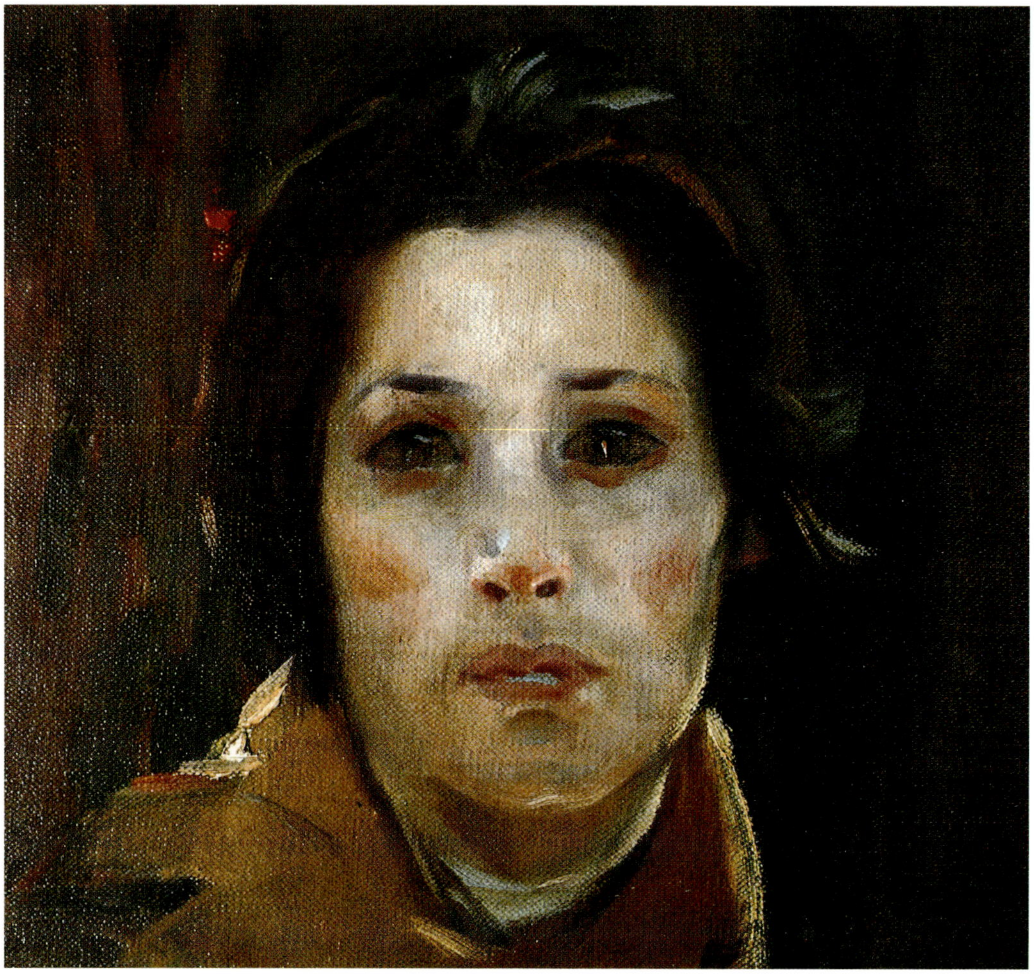

Leopoldo Romañach
STUDY FOR A HEAD–*DETAIL*
1926, Oil on canvas, 19" x 17"
Gift of the Cuban Foundation

detail in this striking image of Cuban mature womanhood. Instead, his bravura brushstroke of "calculated spontaneity" reveals the sitter's nature in a painterly fashion much like the work of Frans Hals, whom Romañach studied throughout his long career. The face of the sitter reveals Romañach's skill in the "new" academic tradition. Layers of carefully applied paint create a face of revealing features where lipstick, rouge, and henna-rinsed hair combine in a portrait of great charm and symbolic presence. G.R.L.

Bibliography:
For a bilingual biography with portrait sketch by Augusto G. Menocal, see *Painting and Sculpture in Cuba* in the National School of Fine Arts San Alejandro, Presidential Palace and National Museum. 1902–1952 Semicentennial of the Independence of Cuba. Havana: Edition of Homage, 1952. Pgs. 71–80.

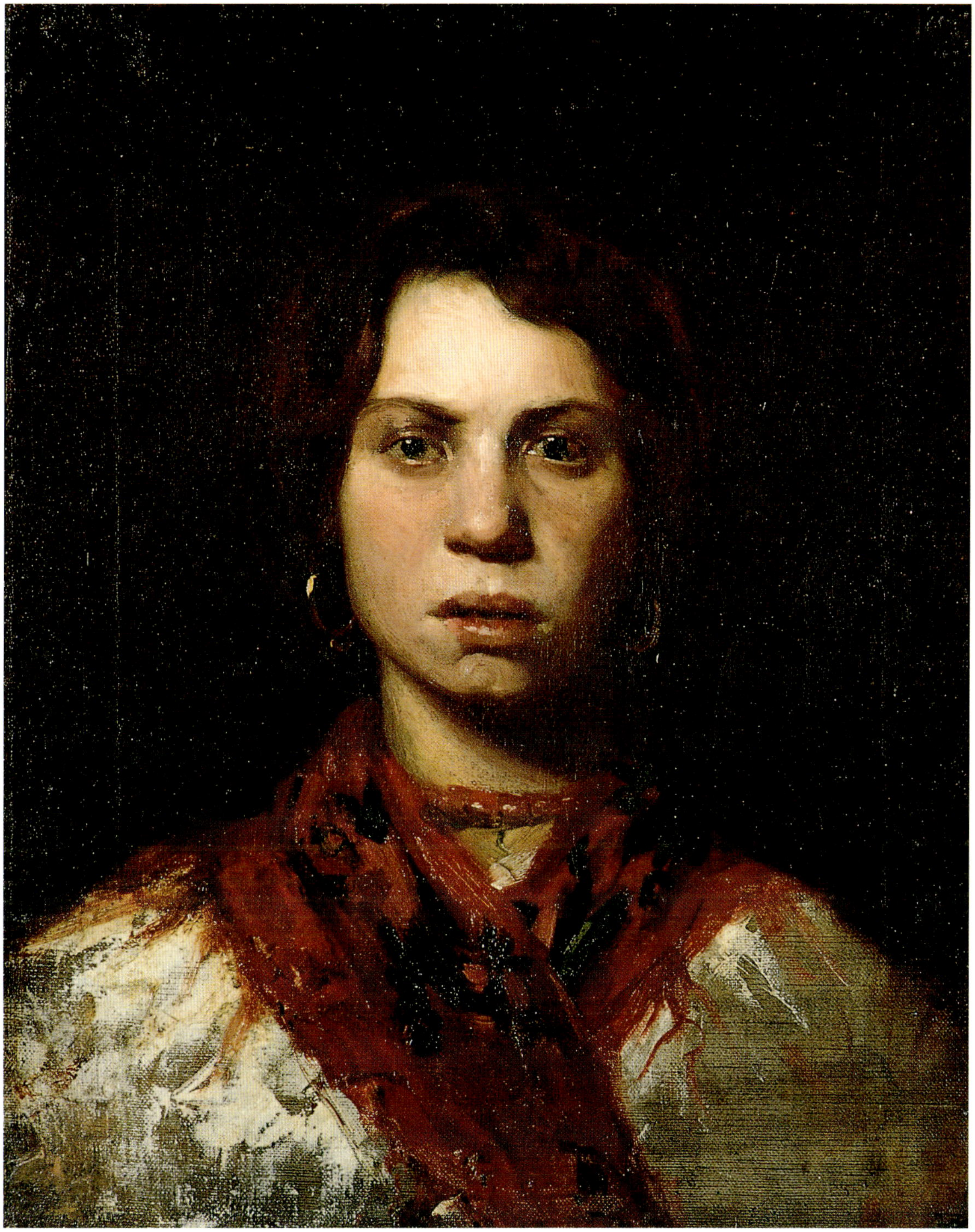

Leopoldo Romañach

ITALIAN PEASANT

Early twentieth century, Oil on canvas, 19" x 15"

Gift of the Cuban Foundation

Armando G. Menocal

1863–1942

Born on July 8, 1863, in Havana, Armando G. Menocal y Menocal was a member of an illustrious Cuban family of political and social importance. Menocal received his early education in the exclusive private schools of Havana. At age seventeen, he completed a certificate in drawing and painting at the Academy of San Alejandro, under the patronage of Miguel Melero.

In 1880, Menocal was sent to Spain to further his education. There he studied under Valencian painter Francisco Jover Casanova, who also taught Pradilla, Domingo, and Joaquin Sorolla y Bastida (1863–1923), the greatest Spanish academic impressionist. In 1884, at the age of twenty-one, Menocal won a second prize in the National Exposition of Madrid.

In 1890, Menocal returned to Cuba where he devoted himself to landscape painting and portraiture. An important controversial painting from this period, *Bobadilla Returns Columbus to Spain,* was praised for its brilliant and intense light, unlike the darker, more traditional Cuban academic formula that relied on Spanish and Italian paradigms.

In 1895, Menocal joined the Cuban revolutionaries fighting against Spanish colonial rule. He served with distinction under the marquis de Santa Lucia and afterward as an aide to General Maximo Gomez. At this time, an important series of pen-and-ink sketches of Cuban revolutionary heroes were sold in the United States by Menocal to help raise funds for the revolutionary cause. An important pen-and-ink portrait of revolutionary leader General Antonio Maceo is part of the permanent collection of the museum in Santiago de Cuba. Menocal served during the entire war and retired as a major in the Revolutionary army.

After the war, Menocal held the chair of painting at San Alejandro. He enjoyed the growing patronage of the Cuban aristocracy and completed several commissions including the decoration of Las Delicias, the mansion of Rosalia Abreu in Palatino. In 1906, Menocal completed one of his masterpieces, *The Death of Maceo*, a Gold Medal winner at the San Francisco Exposition in 1915.

In 1918, when Menocal's cousin Mario G. Menocal became president of Cuba, Armando was given several commissions to decorate the Presidential Palace. There he collaborated with fellow professors from San Alejandro including Antonio Rodriguez Morey, Mariano Miguel, and Esteban Valderrama.

In 1927, Menocal became director of San Alejandro, where he served with distinction as both an administrator and a painter of portraiture and the Cuban landscape.

On September 28, 1942, Menocal died in Havana. He is remembered as a major artistic force and educator in the development of modern Cuban painting.

Menocal's impressionist *Peasant Child*

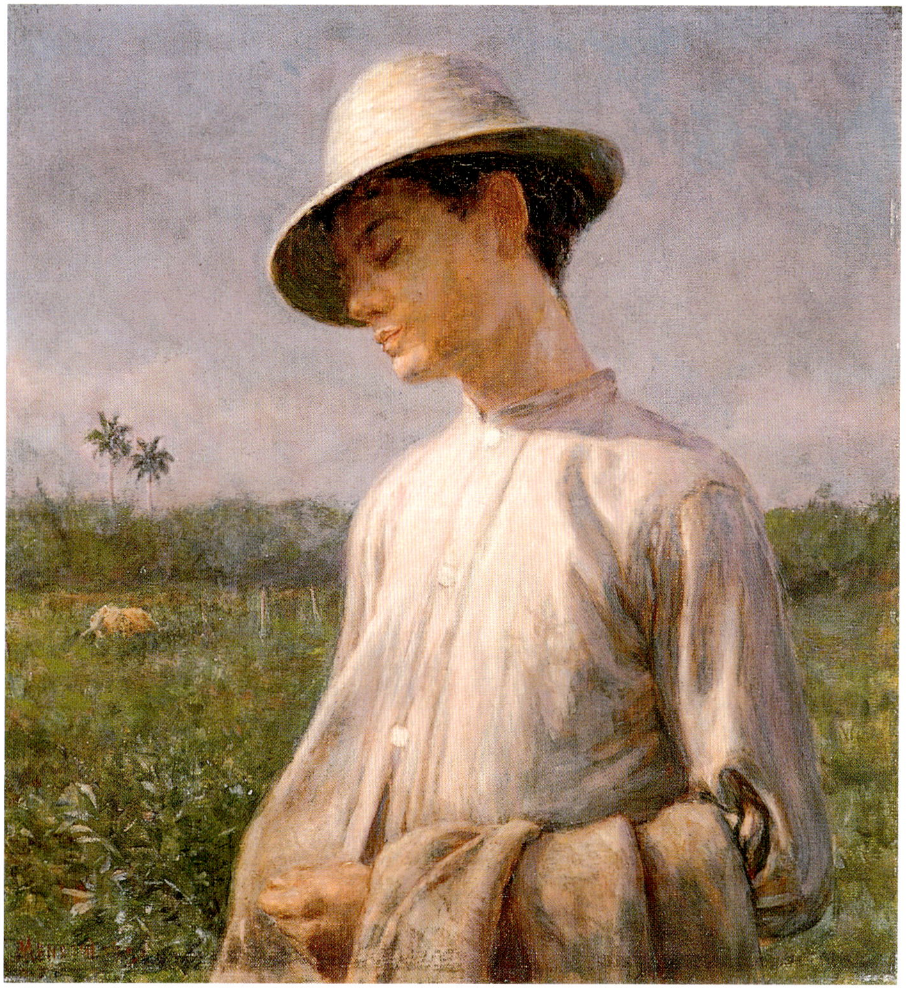

Armando G. Menocal

PEASANT CHILD

1936, Oil on board, 19" x 20"

Gift of the Cuban Foundation

of 1936 summarizes much in the career of this important academic modernist. The color technique made famous by the French impressionists is best seen in the subtle tones of pink, green, and blue of the peasant's white shirt close to the viewer in the foreground and in the painterly brushstroke observed in the treatment of the tropical landscape. The canvas represents an assimilation of contemporary European impressionist technique and design in a painting with a Cuban theme and sensibility. G.R.L.

Bibliography:
For a bilingual biography with portrait sketch by Augusto G. Menocal, see *Painting and Sculpture in Cuba* in the National School of Fine Arts San Alejandro, Presidential Palace and National Museum. 1902–1952 Semicentennial of the Independence of Cuba. Havana: Edition of Homage, 1952. Pgs. 59–66.

Antonio Rodriguez Morey

1874–1930

Born in Havana in 1874, Antonio Rodriguez Morey attended the school Hoyos y Junco of the Sociedad Económica de Amigos del Pais. Later he attended the Institute of the Capital. During this formative period he also studied art at the Academy of San Alejandro.

In 1891, Morey was sent to Europe by his family, and he settled in Florence, Italy. There he pursued his artistic studies at the Professional School of Decorative Arts and later at the Academy of Fine Arts.

In 1895, he moved to Rome where he studied at the Academy of Fine Arts and worked in the studios of José Gallegos and Enrique Serra, two prominent academic painters of the period. He pursued additional training in the studios of Louis Petit and Hermann-David Corrodi. Morey served as professor of drawing and painting for the Institute of the Damas del Sacro Cuoro of Rome.

He returned to Cuba after 1908. In 1912, Morey joined the faculty at San Alejandro where he served successively as professor of drawing, anatomy, perspective, and the history of art. In 1918, he left San Alejandro to become the director of the National Museum of Havana.

Morey exhibited widely in Europe and America, winning a number of important prizes including a Silver Medal in the International Contest of Europe in 1891, a Gold Medal in the San Francisco Exposition of 1915, and a Gold Medal in the Ibero-American Exposition in Seville in 1930.

Morey was also elected as a member of the prestigious Royal Academy of Fine Arts of San Fernando in Madrid. He died in Havana in 1930.

Symphony in Green, painted in 1899 in Rome, represents a high point in the early career of this classically trained academician. Here Morey chooses a damp, dark, and velvety grotto of moss-covered rocks and lush vegetation in low light as his subject. The painting explores the textures and colors of this shady, verdant, quiet scene rendered in precise and minute detail and reflected in the mirror-like waters of a limpid pool which functions as the center of the canvas. *Symphony in Green* is a tour de force example of late nineteenth-century romantic realism reflected in the work of the highly trained young Cuban painter. G.R.L.

Bibliography:
For a bilingual biography with portrait sketch by Augusto G. Menocal, see *Painting and Sculpture in Cuba* in the National School of Fine Arts San Alejandro, Presidential Palace and National Museum. 1902–1952 Semicentennial of the Independence of Cuba. Havana: Edition of Homage, 1952. Pgs. 172–76.

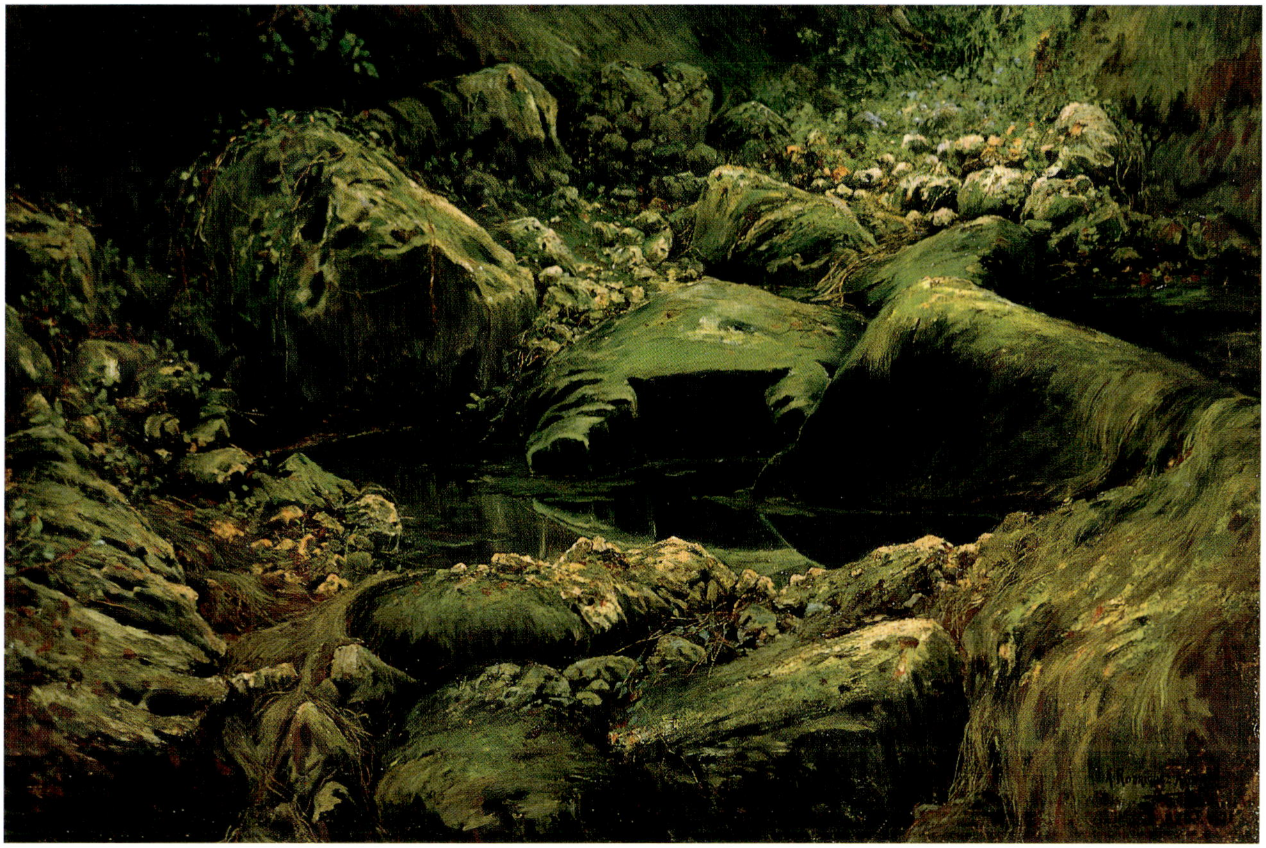

Antonio Rodriguez Morey

SYMPHONY IN GREEN

1899, Oil on canvas, 24" x 36"

Gift of the Cuban Foundation

Juan Gil Garcia

1879–1932

It is extremely ironic that little factual biographical information is known about the life of one of Cuba's most popular painters in the first four decades of the twentieth century. However, Garcia is mentioned anecdotally in many varied sources. In general, he was underappreciated by the Cuban art establishment who saw his work as overly commercial and bourgeois. Because of his skill and sensitivity in drawing and coloration, this author believes Garcia to be the product of formal training in the arts. Recent research sees Garcia at the Valladolid Art School in Spain before his 1899 studies at the Austurias Center in Havana. Whatever his early life provided him, we do know that after 1920 he enjoyed a great popularity as a painter of still lifes and picturesque views of Havana and its environs. Juan Gil Garcia was born in Madrid, Spain, in 1879 and emigrated to Cuba in 1899. He died in Havana in 1932. We also know that today his still lifes are among the most accomplished and suggestive of all academic works in the realistic tradition in the twentieth century in Cuba. It has been argued that no middle-class living room in Cuba was without a Garcia still life. Garcia was so popular an artist that four of his fruit still lifes were printed as lithographs and sold a startling 50,000 copies each. While Antonio Sánchez Araujo (1887–1946) painted statuesque still life arrangements of inanimate objects in a cool and formal manner usually in a stark indefinite interior space, Garcia's still lifes are warm and sensuous and usually set outdoors as an extension of nature. Moreover, where many academics of the period emphasized the Cézanne-like formal order of the universe, expressed in arrangements of everyday objects, Garcia seemed more occupied with exploring the sentient world where carefully selected and referential delectables appealed to the senses and the emotions of the growing Cuban middle class.

In *Still Life with Oranges, Cocoanut, Cashew Apples, Canistel, White Sapote and Mamoncillos* and *Still Life with Mangoes and Sweet Apples*, both completed in 1932, Garcia increases the surface texture and sensuous quality by first violating the external forms through slicing and peeling selected items. He then increases the catalog of tropical fruits he presents to the viewer in an enlivened outdoor setting with exotic color and dramatic light. In both compositions, Garcia also seems preoccupied with suggestive biomorphic shapes and forms that refer to the similarities between the worlds of botany and biology. Here also, the extreme close-up perspective invites the viewer to fully appreciate and savor these lush tropical edibles through their exotic shapes, textures, and seductive colors, heightened by their placement directly on the uncovered ground as they suggestively spill out of their woven baskets.

In many ways, Garcia's still lifes can be understood as skillfully executed bourgeois salutations to life where the material world, like life itself, is viewed as transitory, ephemeral, beautiful, and fragile as the flowers of the field or the tasty and symbolic fruits of the earth. G.R.L.

Bibliography:
Gary R. Libby. "Still Lively After All These Years," *Arts and Sciences Magazine*, Spring 1993.
Jorge Regal. *Apuntes Sobre La Pintura y El Grabado en Cuba*. Havana: Editorial Letras Cubanas, 1982. Pgs. 274–77.

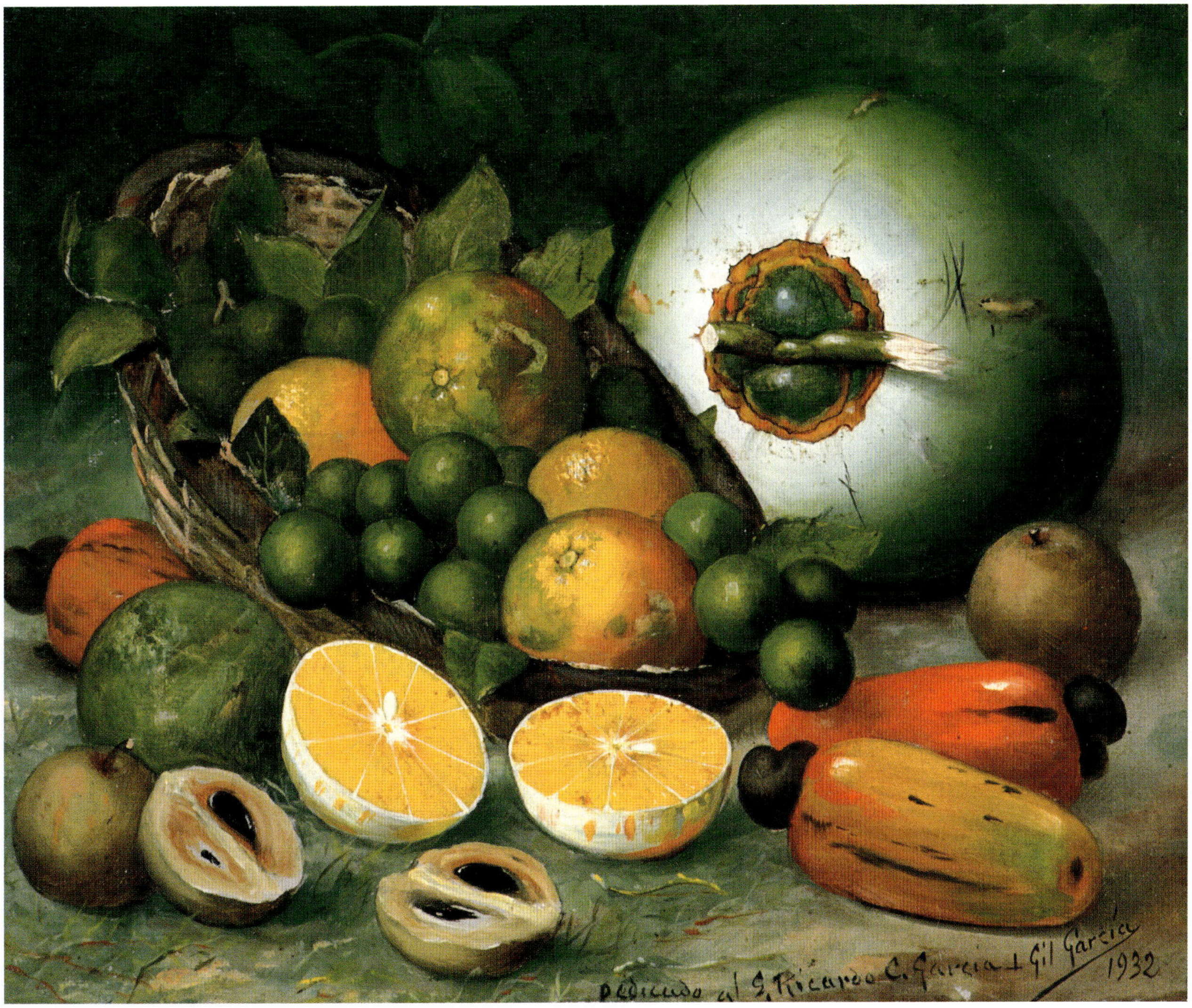

Juan Gil Garcia

STILL LIFE WITH ORANGES, COCOANUT, CASHEW APPLES, CANISTEL, WHITE SAPOTE AND MAMONCILLOS

1932, Oil on canvas, 14" x 17"

Gift of Elias Drymonis

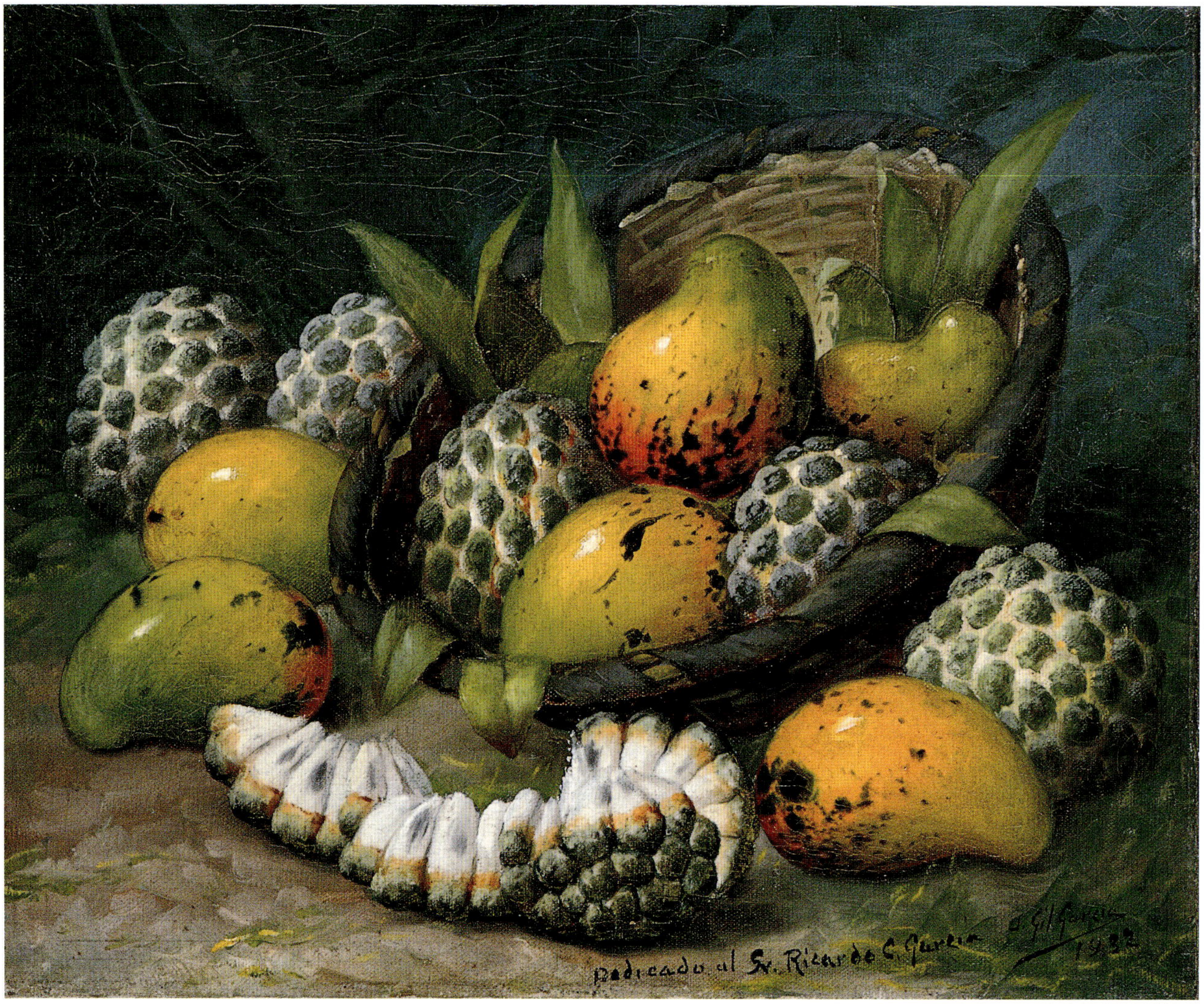

Juan Gil Garcia

STILL LIFE WITH MANGOES AND SWEET APPLES

1932, Oil on canvas, 14" x 17"

Gift of Elias Drymonis

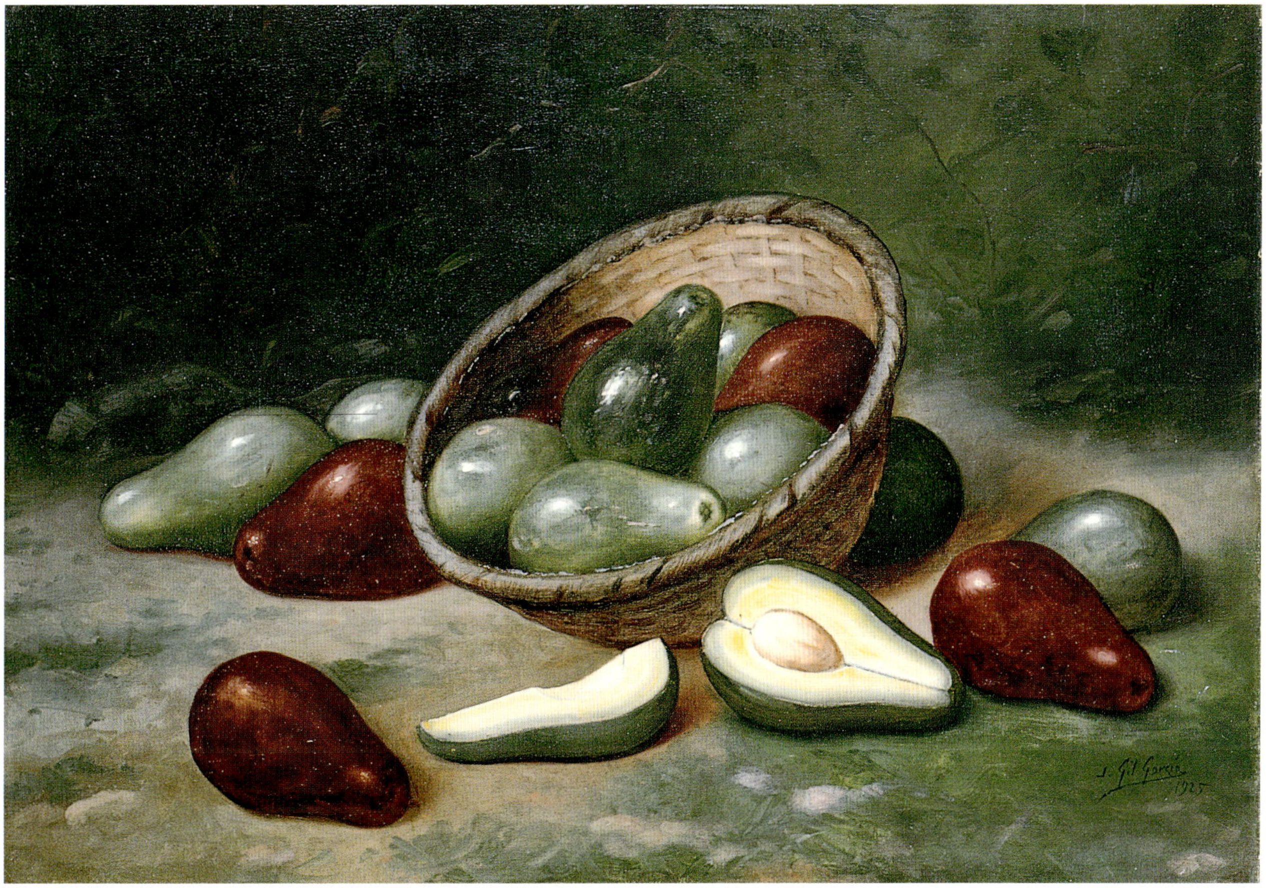

Juan Gil Garcia

Avocado Pears

1925, Oil on canvas, 25" x 37"

Gift of the Cuban Foundation

Concepción Ferrant

1882–1969

Born on February 28, 1882, in Guanabacao, Havana, Concepción Ferrant y Gomez was educated in Havana, where she later studied art at the National School of Fine Arts.

In 1918, she received scholarships enabling her to study at both the Art Students League and the National Academy of Design in New York. She then left for Spain where she continued her studies and exhibited her work.

In 1924, Ferrant returned to Cuba where twenty-six works in her inaugural exhibition in the galleries of the National Association of Painters and Sculptors in Havana received rave reviews.

Throughout her career, Ferrant won a number of important prizes including the Special Prize of the National Academy of Design, New York, 1920; the Gold Medal at the Ibero-American Exposition in Seville, 1930; and the Gold Medal from the Fine Arts Club, Havana, 1940. Ferrant also authored several books on literature and art, including the popular *Art Anatomy.*

In 1926, Concepción Ferrant joined the faculty of the Academy of San Alejandro as assistant professor of art anatomy. During her tenure at the National School of Fine Arts, she exhibited in Cuba, North America, and Europe until 1950. She was also made a life member of the League of American Artists. She died in Havana.

The Child of the Artist, 1918, is a colorful and painterly portrait of her son, with shoulder-length black hair, large brown eyes, and a fair complexion. He wears a formal white shirt buttoned at the neck and a luxurious purple cravat as he looks at the viewer. To the left is an artist's table with paint and brushes. The midground behind the boy is filled by an easel with a large painting by Ferrant of a white dove and a nude, probably Ferrant's favorite model, Salome, who appears in many paintings from this period. The brushstroke is loose, illustrating the relaxed nature of the new academic styles after the influence of European modernism. Ferrant's colors are bright, highly saturated, and vibrant, creating a convincing convexity of the youthful subject full of artistic promise against the dark indefinite background of the artist's studio. G.R.L.

Bibliography:
For a bilingual biography with portrait sketch by Augusto G. Menocal, see *Painting and Sculpture in Cuba* in the National School of Fine Arts San Alejandro, Presidential Palace and National Museum. 1902–1952 Semicentennial of the Independence of Cuba. Havana: Edition of Homage, 1952. Pgs. 181–82.

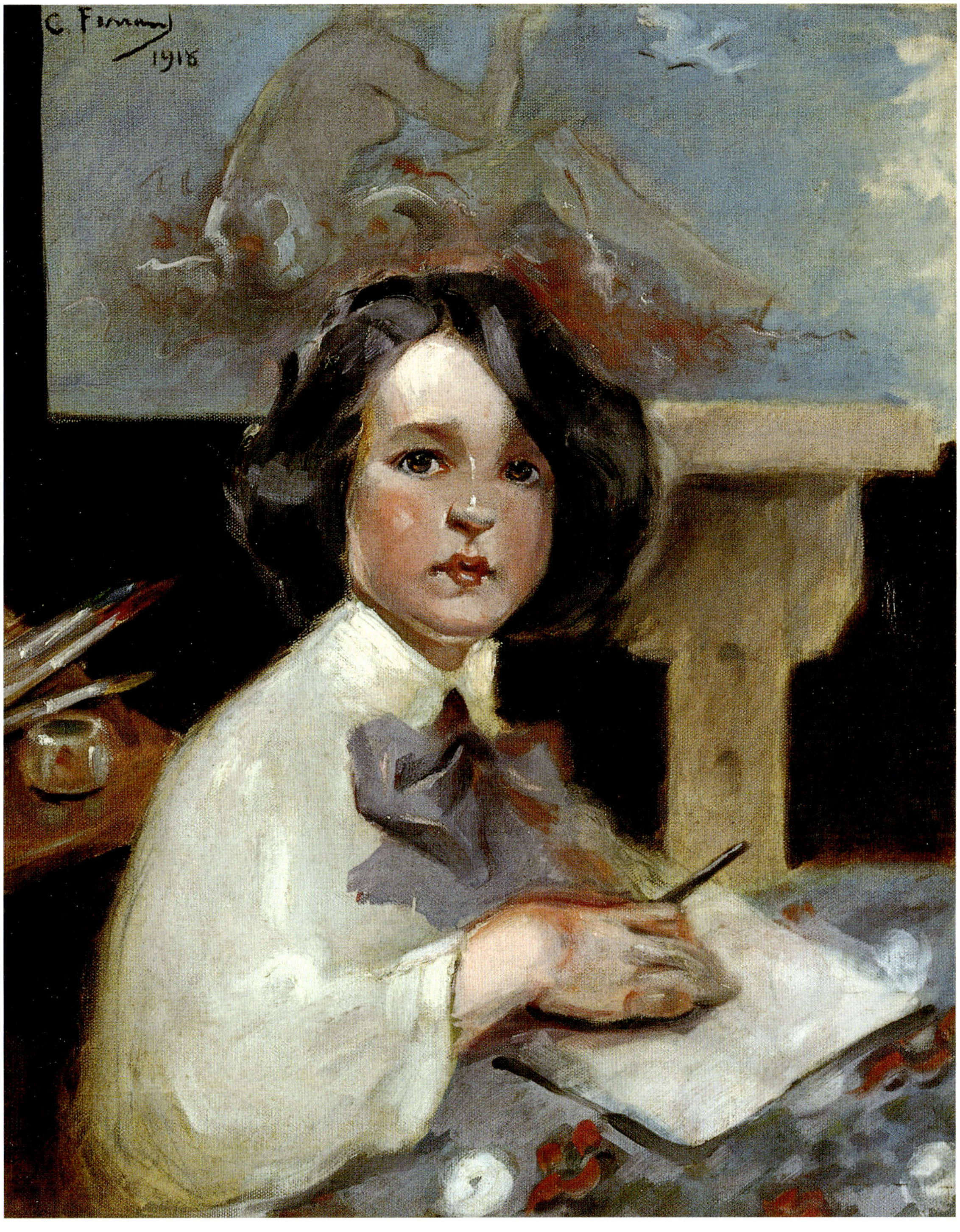

Concepción Ferrant

The Child of the Artist

1918, Oil on canvas, 24" x 20"

Gift of the Cuban Foundation

Mariano Miguel

1885–1954

Born in Madrid, Spain, in 1885, Mariano Miguel González was an important writer, journalist, and painter who eventually became the director of the Academy of San Alejandro, the National School of Art in Cuba.

After completing a traditional education in Madrid, Miguel moved to Paris in 1900. In 1901, he returned to Madrid to become an illustrator. There he worked on several important publications until 1904, when he arrived in Havana to work as an illustrator for the newspaper *La Discusión*. Until 1908, Miguel served as art director for several influential daily and weekly journals including *El Figaro*, *Bohemia*, *La Politica Comica*, and *Mundo Illustrato*.

In 1908, Miguel returned to Spain where he edited several significant art and cultural magazines in Madrid. He continued to study painting by attending the studio of Cecilio Plá, a popular academic painter of the period known for his mural decorations at the Casino de Madrid.

In 1910, Miguel returned to Cuba and he joined the staff of *Diario de la Marina*. He eventually became art editor and cultural critic. In 1912, Miguel became a Cuban citizen and continued to work in cultural areas of the Cuban press. He also founded an ill-fated weekly, *Actualidades*. In 1919, Miguel joined the faculty of San Alejandro, where he first served as assistant professor of landscape painting and then, as full professor of elementary drawing and modeling.

In 1928, at the academy, he urged the creation of the Chair of Engraving and served as its first professor. Miguel excelled in the process of printmaking. However, he introduced everyday domestic themes and popular subject matter, which proved to be controversial for polite Cuban society.

He also continued to paint. He was one of the first Cuban artists to celebrate the city of Trinidad de Cuba, where he captured urban views of this colonial city founded by Don Diego Velázquez in 1515.

Miguel exhibited widely and won prizes in Cuba, Spain, the United States, and Mexico, including a Silver Medal in the Philadelphia Exposition of 1926 and a Gold Medal at the Ibero-American Exposition in Seville in 1930.

In 1920, Miguel returned to Madrid to establish a studio. In 1923, he was appointed an Academician of the Royal Galician Academy. In 1948, he was made a member of the National Academy of Arts and Letters in Havana. He died in Havana in 1954.

His large and impressive oil on canvas *La Popa*, 1923, captures the important pilgrimage church in Santiago de Cuba, from the bottom of the long processional stairs, now lost, but captured forever in the painting. By positioning the viewer at the bottom of the steps, Miguel also suggests the long climb in life to the church, the symbol of the house of God. The large brushstrokes and skillful use of impasto give this colorful and spatial cityscape a boldness and

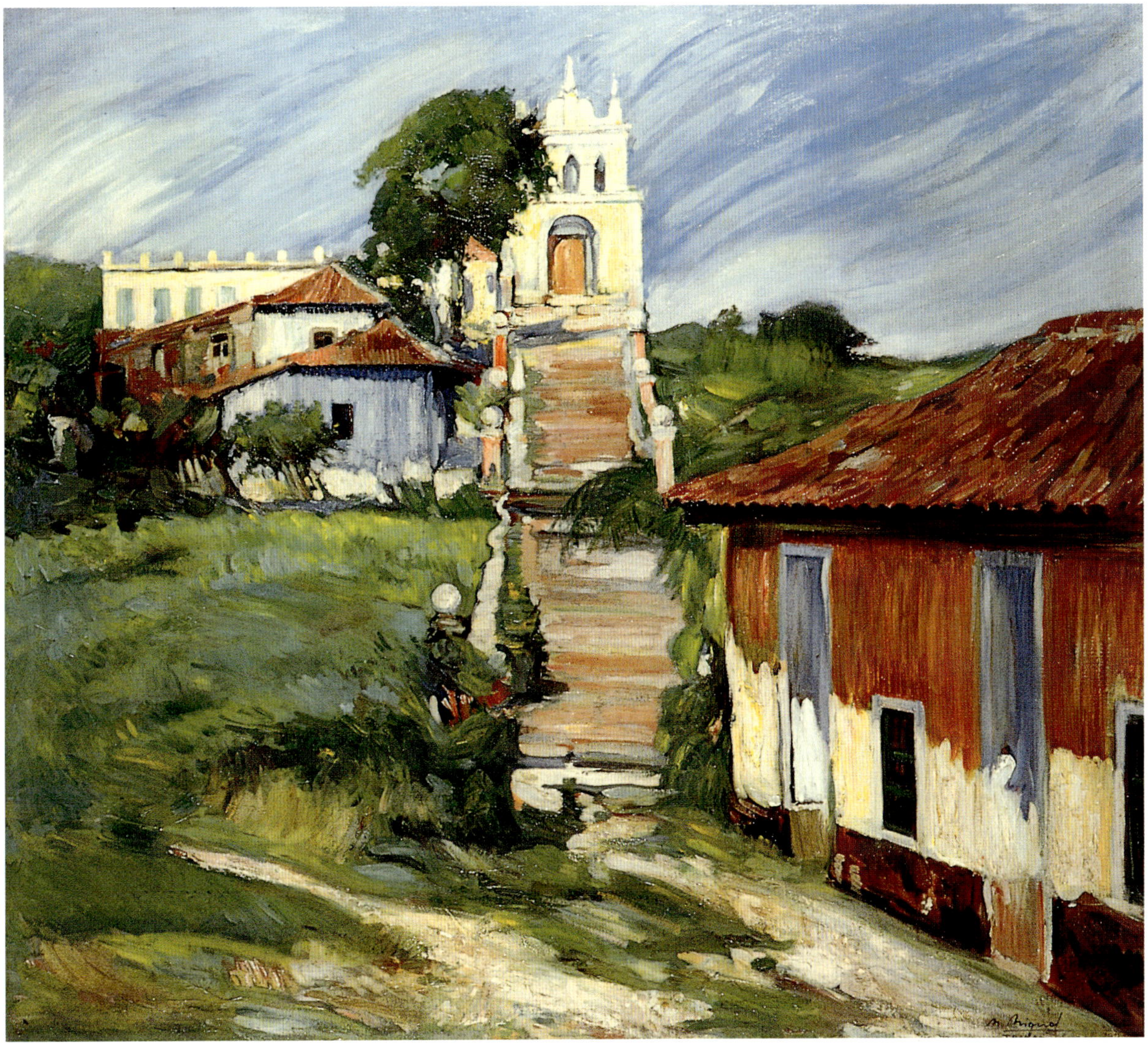

Mariano Miguel

La Popa

1923, Oil on canvas, 41" x 51"

Gift of the Cuban Foundation

energy amplified in the deep blue sky, the dark red tile roof of an adjacent townhouse, and the strong diagonals, verticals, and horizontals of the dynamic composition. G.R.L.

Bibliography:
For a bilingual biography with portrait sketch by Augusto G. Menocal, see *Painting and Sculpture in Cuba* in the National School of Fine Arts San Alejandro, Presidential Palace and National Museum. 1902–1952 Semicentennial of the Independence of Cuba. Havana: Edition of Homage, 1952. Pgs. 120–26.

Antonio Sánchez Araujo

1887–1946

Born in Santa Lucia, Oriente Province, in 1887, Antonio Sánchez Araujo began his serious study of art in 1907, at the National School of Fine Arts in Havana. Later, he won a five-year scholarship that allowed him to study in Barcelona, Madrid, and Paris, where Araujo copied and recopied the Renaissance masterpieces at the Louvre. He also attended formal classes in the Academy Colarossi and the Grande Chaumiere in Paris.

Araujo returned to Cuba where he exhibited his work in Havana in 1925, after a distinguished career in exhibitions throughout Europe and the United States, including one-man exhibitions in Barcelona and Madrid. He also exhibited selected works in group exhibitions in Madrid in 1920 and 1921, San Francisco, in 1925; Philadelphia, in 1926; Baltimore, and Seville, in 1930. He won a Bronze Medal in the Sesquicentennial Exposition in Philadelphia in 1926 and a Gold Medal in Seville, in 1930.

Araujo was director of the Free School of Plastic Arts in the Association of Painters and Sculptors in Havana from 1926 to 1929. In 1926, he also joined the faculty of San Alejandro as full professor of ancient Greek drawing. He served on the faculty at San Alejandro until his death on October 13, 1946, at the age of fifty-nine.

Araujo's *Still Life* of ca. 1940 captures eleven objects on a dark table surface against an indefinite shallow wall. Most of the composition occupies the foreground with slightly tilted objects conceived as geometric shapes in white, blue, green, and brown. The subject matter in the left foreground, presented to the viewer of the painting, is a frugal repast of smoked fish, bread, and wine arranged together in the right midground with a large ceramic jug, soupbowl on edge, smaller bowl, wine bottle, and knife. All of the objects are representational, and their shapes are accentuated by a soft raking light coming from the right side of the composition, casting shadows in a modest chiaroscuro. The paint surface is smooth with the exception of a white impasto on the inside of the wine cup. Araujo's *Still Life* illustrates the artist's late preoccupation and flirtation with the surrealism of the Italians, Morandi and de Chirico, yet translated through the mind of a conservative Cuban academician concerned with a Cézanne-like order of form, texture, and light. G.R.L.

Bibliography:
For a bilingual biography with portrait sketch by Augusto G. Menocal, see *Painting and Sculpture in Cuba* in the National School of Fine Arts San Alejandro, Presidential Palace and National Museum. 1902–1952 Semicentennial of the Independence of Cuba. Havana: Edition of Homage, 1952. Pgs. 133–34.

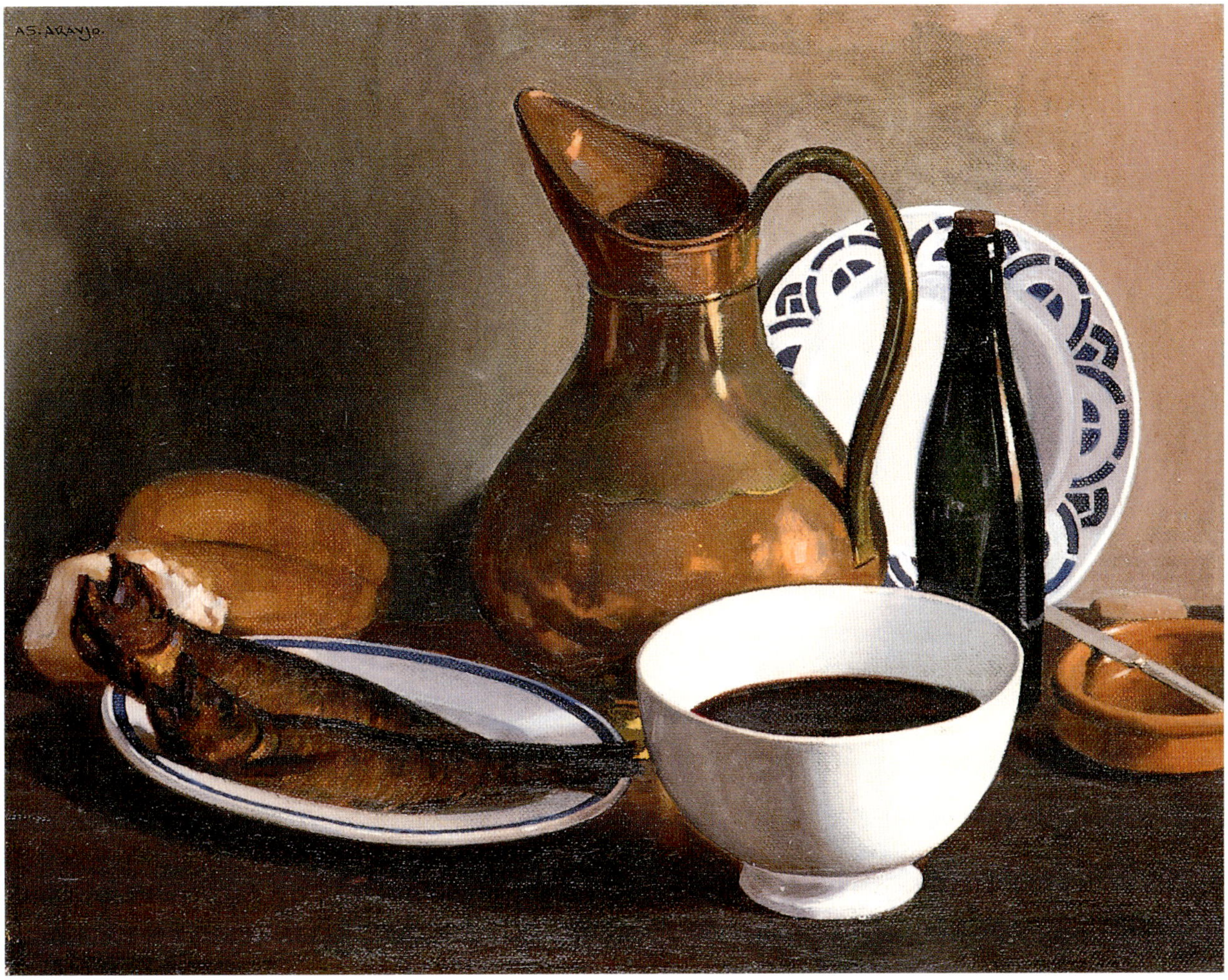

Antonio Sánchez Araujo

STILL LIFE

Ca. 1940, Oil on canvas, 19" x 25"

Gift of the Cuban Foundation

Eduardo Abela

1889–1965

Eduardo Abela was born in San Antonio de los Baños, Havana province, in 1889 and died in the city of Havana in 1965. He graduated as a painter from the Academy of San Alejandro in 1921 and lived in Madrid (1921–24) and Paris (1927–29), furthering his artistic education. In Paris, he developed his first mature style in a body of expressionist drawings and paintings about Afro-Cuban popular culture. During the 1930s Abela kept busy working as a cartoonist, painter, art administrator, and cultural attaché. He went through a second mature phase in the late 1930s when he started working in larger, more naturalistic paintings about the Cuban countryside. Abela's artistic language went through yet another transformation in the 1950s when he developed a kind of magic-expressionism representing a fantasy world populated by women, children, and animals. He won purchase awards at the 1938 and 1956 National Salons, and his paintings are well represented in the National Museum in Havana. His paintings are also found in private collections in Cuba, the United States, Spain, and France.

Promenade is an excellent example of Abela's third stylistic phase, ca.1950 to 1964. Using a sophisticated cartoon-like drawing, rich pigmented surface, and soft arbitrary colors, he creates an enchanting fairy tale world. In this case a horse-drawn carriage with a small but venerable looking passenger rides with an entourage through an ill-defined rural landscape. The image has a dreamy carnival-like appearance, and its small scale invites intimate viewing. J.A.M.

Bibliography:

Abela, Magia y Fabulas. (Exhibition catalogue) Bilingual essays by Guy Pérez Cisneros (reprint), Humberto Medrano, Alfredo Lozano, and Luis Lastra. Miami: Museo Cubano de Arte y Cultura, 1984

José Seoane Gallo. *Eduardo Abela cerca del cerco*. Havana: Editorial Letras Cubanas, 1986.

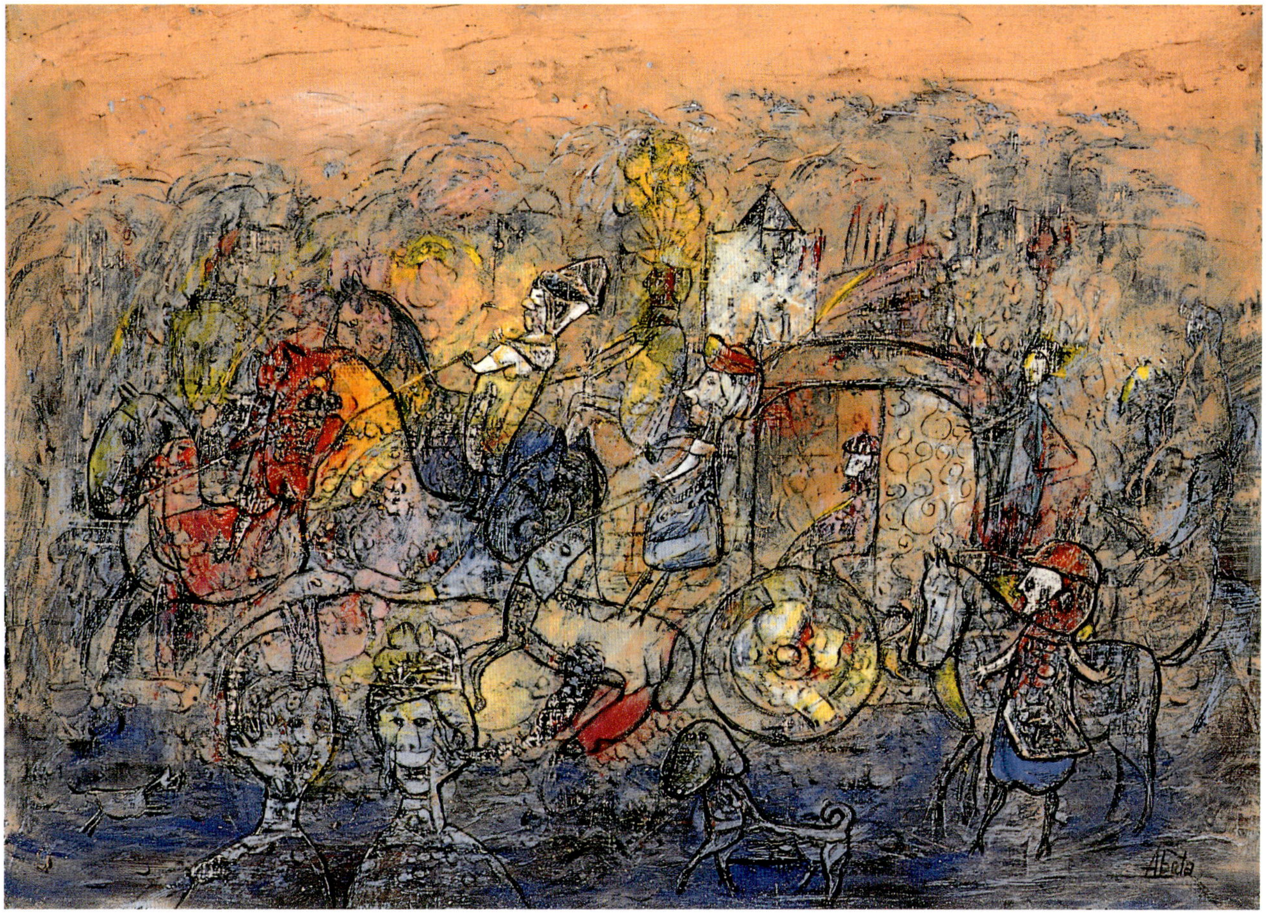

Eduardo Abela

PROMENADE

Ca. 1950, Mixed media on board, 14" x 20"

Gift of the Cuban Foundation

José A. Bencomo Mena

1890–1962

Born in Remedios, Las Villas province, Cuba, in 1890, José A. Bencomo Mena finished both his elementary and secondary education there. He then traveled to Havana where he studied painting and drawing at the Academy of San Alejandro. Bencomo Mena received the highest score in the graduation examinations at the Academy, allowing him a Cuban national scholarship to pursue his studies in Europe, where he settled in Rome after a brief stay in Florence. While in Florence, he studied etching, wood engraving, and mural painting at the Institute of Decorative Arts and took advanced art history classes at Florence University. Like several of his predecessors in France and Italy, Bencomo Mena studied and drew from corpses at the Florence Hospital. In Rome, he studied fresco techniques at the Encaustic School and visited the city's museums, especially the collections of the Vatican. He exhibited selectively in both Rome and Florence.

Bencomo Meno returned to Cuba in 1927. He exhibited widely in Cuba after his first one-man exhibition in the Salon of the Diario de la Marina in 1928, the year he joined the faculty of the Academy of San Alejandro as assistant professor. José A. Bencomo Mena died in Havana.

The large and impressive *Keeper of the Roosters* is dated 1934. The canvas captures a middle-aged cockfighter sitting on a bench dressed in a textured gray suit and bright red scarf as he lovingly holds and grooms two of his fighting roosters. The dark interior is brightened by a light blue pitcher in the right midground and melons and greens to the left. Brushstroke is generally loose with a painterly quality in the expressive and smiling face of the central figure as a strong light from the left animates the scene with a bold chiaroscuro. Less formally academic than most paintings from this period, *Keeper of the Roosters* illustrates the growing and serious influence of Cuban folk art in the development of modern Cuban painting. G.R.L.

Bibliography:
For a bilingual biography with portrait sketch by Augusto G. Menocal, see *Painting and Sculpture in Cuba* in the National School of Fine Arts San Alejandro, Presidential Palace and National Museum. 1902–1952 Semicentennial of the Independence of Cuba. Havana: Edition of Homage, 1952. Pgs. 189–90.

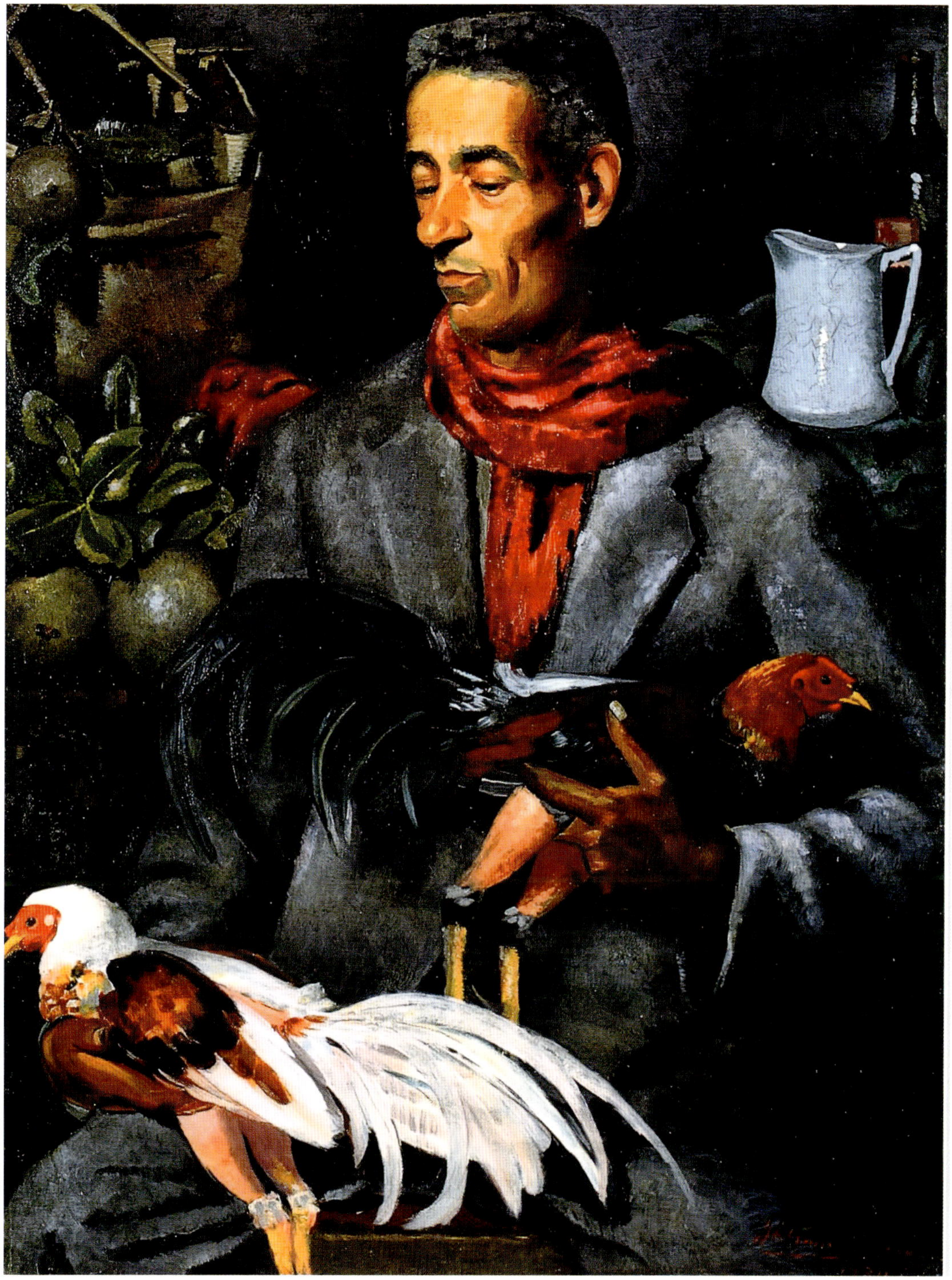

José A. Bencomo Mena
Keeper of the Roosters
1934, Oil on canvas, 38" x 29"
Gift of the Cuban Foundation

Emilio Rivero Merlin

1890–1977

Born in Güira de Melena, Havana, on November 18, 1890, Emilio Rivero Merlin was an accomplished landscape painter and portraitist known for his brilliant color harmonies and accomplished technique.

In 1916, he received a scholarship from the city of Havana to attend the Academy of San Alejandro where he studied for four years. At age twenty he traveled abroad visiting Italy before settling in Madrid where he attended the Royal Academy of Fine Arts of San Fernando. In 1921, additional scholarships allowed him to study with Manolo Mantilla and Pastor Argudín, two important Cuban artists working in Madrid. Merlin then toured Spain for two years sketching in Dovadonga, Luanco, Oviedo, Villaviciosa, Gijón, and Granada. Merlin produced 190 paintings during the period. Many of Merlin's paintings joined important collections in Puerto Rico, the United States, where Gloria Vanderbilt purchased *Triste Paseo*, Cuba, and Spain.

In 1923, during a painting trip to Morocco, Merlin performed in the Spanish film *Sun of Justice*, which showed in Havana after Merlin returned to Cuba in 1924. He moved to Mexico where he perfected his portrait style through a series of commissions including General Calles, the president of Mexico, and Francisco Serrano, the governor of the state of Mexico.

In 1928, after the death of his father, Merlin returned to Cuba. During this period he returned to landscape and genre painting, including patriotic subjects from Cuban history.

Emilio Rivero Merlin was a prolific painter who enjoyed an important reputation throughout Cuba, the United States, where he exhibited in New York, Baltimore, Philadelphia, Key West, and San Francisco; Mexico, Argentina, and Spain, where he exhibited in Seville, Granada, Barcelona, and Madrid.

In 1934, he joined the faculty as professor of the Elementary School of San Alejandro. An accomplished academician, he won the Gold Medal in Seville and Bronze Medals in Havana in major national exhibitions. He died in Havana.

The large and colorful *Corner in a Cuban Garden* probably dates from after 1930, when Merlin began to paint extraordinary private garden views, appreciated for their brilliant color, draughtsmanship, and sense of quietude.

In the painting, Merlin captures a private walled garden resplendent with large philodendron and bougainvillea enlivened by a white hot light that flows through the doorway and over loose bricks like golden lava. The detailed drawing of the elephant ears is in contrast to the loose brushstroke of the thick vegetation and brilliant red bougainvillea vine seen in the trees and in full bloom framed in the doorway of the silent and private garden whose intimacy is made accessible to the viewer by the painting. G.R.L.

Bibliography:
For a bilingual biography with portrait sketch by Augusto G. Menocal, see *Painting and Sculpture in Cuba* in the National School of Fine Arts San Alejandro, Presidential Palace and National Museum. 1902–1952 Semicentennial of the Independence of Cuba. Havana: Edition of Homage, 1952. Pgs. 200–02.

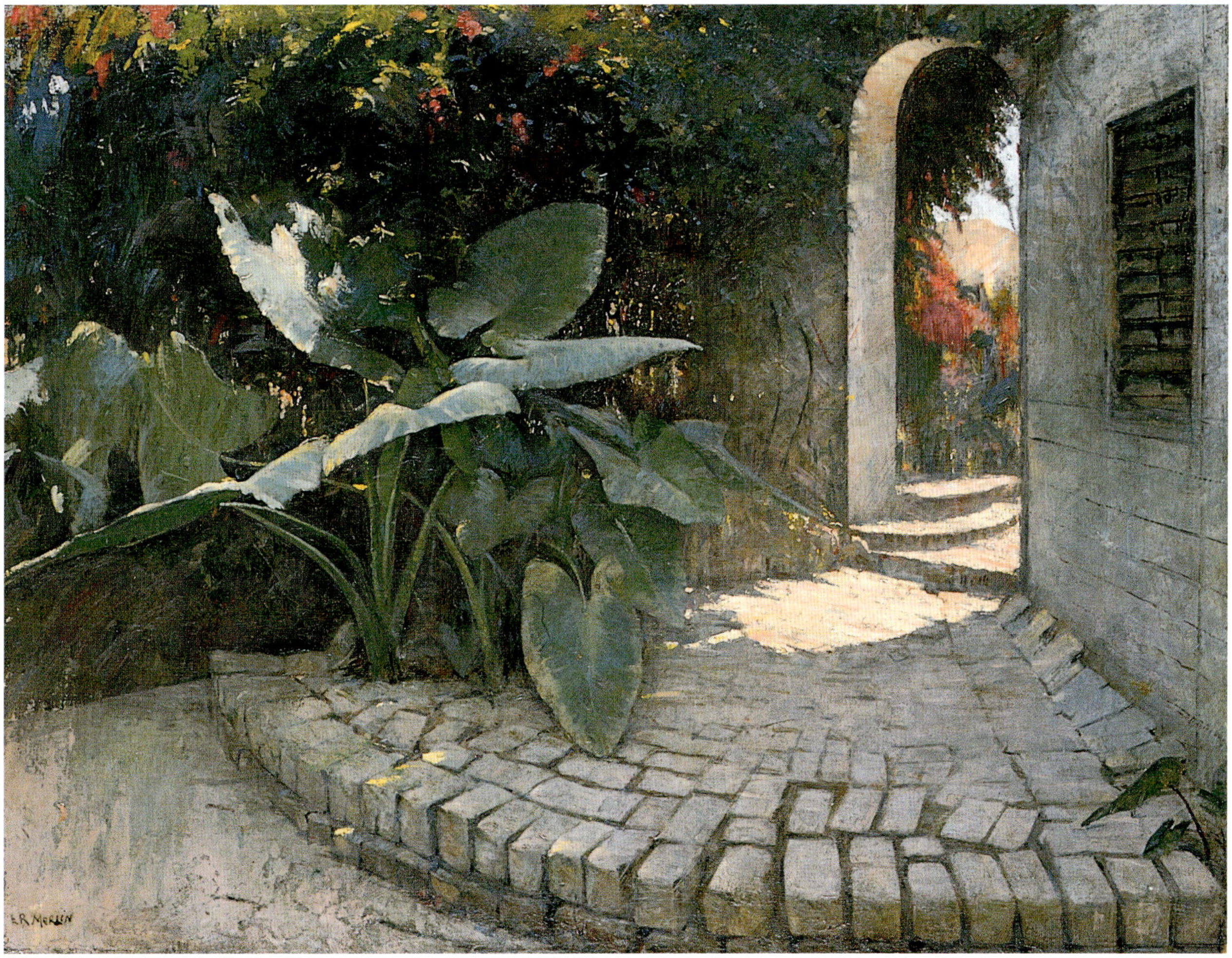

Emilio Rivero Merlin

CORNER IN A CUBAN GARDEN

1930, Oil on canvas, 30" x 39"

Gift of the Cuban Foundation

Esteban Valderrama

1892–1964

Born on March 16, 1892, in the city of Matanzas, Esteban Valderrama y Peña was descended from a family of Cuban patriots. In 1897, his father, Major Esteban Valderrama y López, an officer in the Army of the Revolution, died, leaving the young Esteban and his two siblings under the care of their mother, Doña Landelina Peña y del Pino.

Valderrama finished his early education in Matanzas. In 1906, he won a scholarship from the provincial government to attend the Academy of San Alejandro in Havana. In 1908, Valderrama finished his studies with the highest grades and was sent, on scholarship, to the Royal Academy of Fine Arts of San Fernando in Madrid. Valderrama studied there for two years. In 1911, he moved to Paris and entered the National School of Fine Arts as a special student due to his high competitive scores on the entrance exams. He studied painting, drawing, and sculpture in Paris until 1914, when he returned to Havana to join the staff of *El Heraldo de Cuba*, as portrait artist for the Sunday supplement.

In 1915, Valderrama received an award from the National Academy of Arts in Havana for his three canvas painting *Fundamental*. Later in 1915, he won a Bronze Medal in the Panama Pacific International Exposition for a pastel portrait, *General Menocal*. Valderrama won awards throughout his long career including a Gold Medal in Seville in 1930. In 1942, he received a major commission to decorate the Presidential Palace of Cuba. These allegorical and historical murals are generally considered his masterpieces. Valderrama also painted portraits. In 1940, he completed his masterful portrait of Franklin Delano Roosevelt commissioned by the Cuban Senate. In 1945, he completed a life-size portrait of José Martí for the Cuban embassy in Mexico City later given by the Cuban government to General Avila Camacho, president of Mexico.

Valderrama joined the faculty of San Alejandro in 1918 at the age of twenty-six. He served in different professorships there until his retirement after the revolution of 1959. Also an author, Valderrama wrote an important text, *La Perspective y el Espacio,* in 1935. At the time of the revolution, Valderrama was considered an important link between the academicians of the nineteenth and twentieth centuries.

The Park of the Brother-hood in Havana is a bright public commissioned work from 1957. Painted in a flat colorist palette, the oil captures a group of uniformed adults in the left foreground holding a Cuban flag and a banner celebrating nineteenth- century revolutionary hero Maximo Gomez. Women in the right midground sit on the wall of the Park monument, which surrounds a large tree that functions as one of the implied symbolic subjects of the painting. A clear blue sky is accentuated by soft cumulus clouds in this celebration of Cuban civic life. G.R.L.

Bibliography:
For a bilingual biography with portrait sketch by Augusto G. Menocal, see *Painting and Sculpture in Cuba* in the National School of Fine Arts San Alejandro, Presidential Palace and National Museum. 1902–1952 Semicentennial of the Independence of Cuba. Havana: Edition of Homage, 1952. Pgs. 84–96

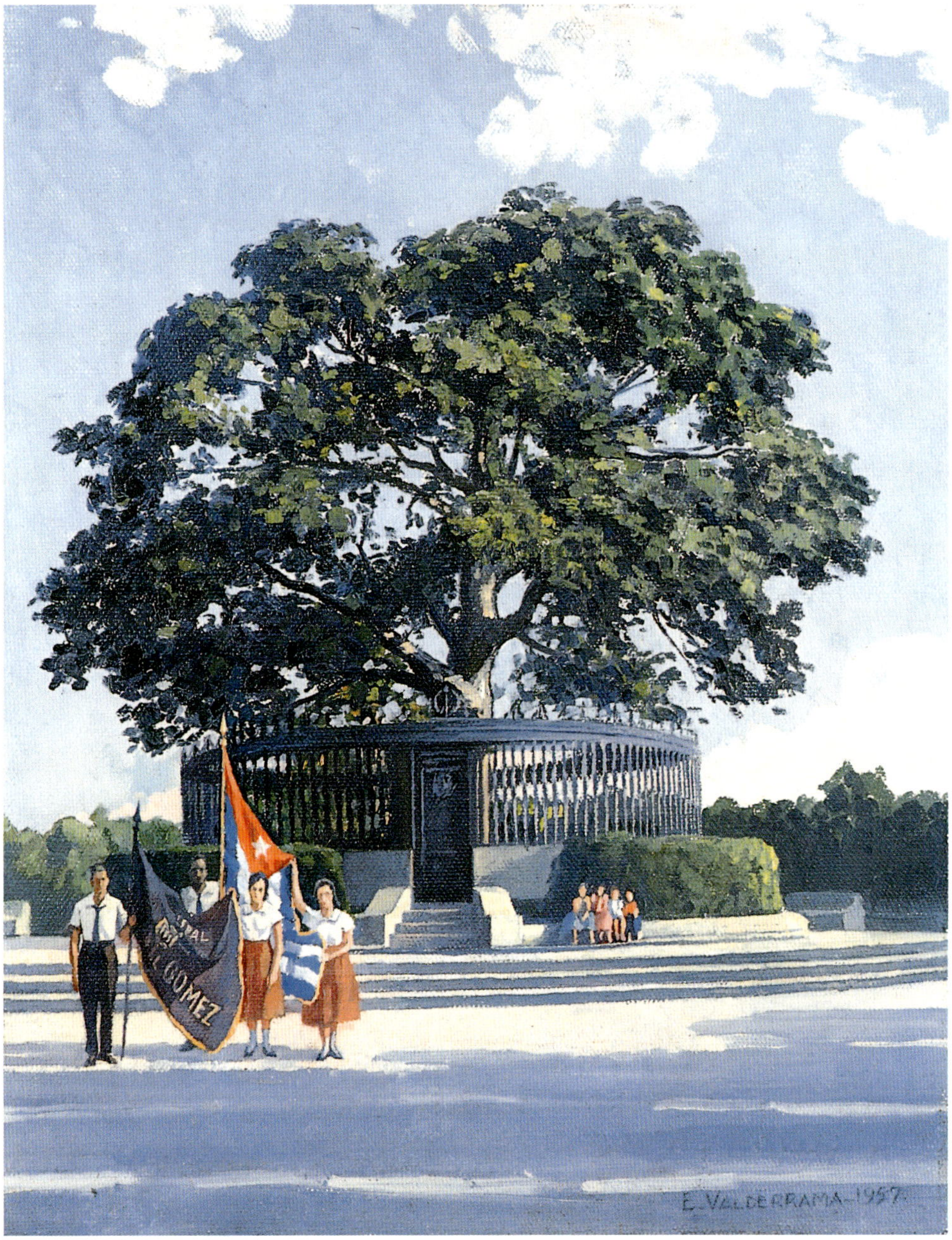

Esteban Valderrama

The Park of The Brotherhood in Havana

1957, Oil on canvas, 22" x 18"

Gift of the Cuban Foundation

Amelia Peláez

1896–1968

Amelia Peláez y del Casal was born in Yaguajay, province of Las Villas, in 1896 and died in Havana in 1968. She graduated in painting from the Academy of San Alejandro in 1924 and continued her artistic education in Paris from 1927 to 1934. She developed her mature style in the second half of the 1930s in Havana, when she adapted aspects of the art of Matisse, Braque, Picasso, and Alexandra Exter to interpret her immediate environment, particularly Havana's colonial architecture and her garden fruits and flowers, as symbols of personal and collective ethos. In the 1940s her still lifes became more complex in form and brilliant in color, while in the 1950s they turned in the opposite direction toward simpler forms and color schemes. The last decade of her life she returned to the "baroque" compositions and stained-glass-like colors of the 1940s period. Peláez won awards at the National Salons of 1935, 1938, 1956, and 1959. She exhibited extensively during her lifetime and was the subject of major retrospective exhibitions at the Museo Nacional in Havana (1968), the Cuban Museum of Art and Culture in Miami (1988), and the Museo de Bellas Artes in Caracas (1991). In the United States, her paintings are in the collections of the Museum of Modern Art in New York, the Art Museum of the Americas in Washington, D.C., and in numerous private collections.

Still Life of 1955 is representative of Peláez's work of that decade, when she came close to the aesthetics of geometric abstraction and its belief in the purification of form and color, while never abandoning her expressive subject matter. In this painting a centrally placed flower set in an architectural interior is suggested with the abstract economy of a hieroglyphic, but not its cold precision. The image for all of its rational, constructed quality, it is also strongly intuitive and expressionistic.

J.A.M.

Bibliography:
Amelia Pélaez, 1896–1968. (Exhibition catalogue) Essay by Giulio Blanc. Miami: Museo Cubano de Arte y Cultura, 1988.

Amelia Peláez, exposición retrospectiva, 1924–1967. (Exhibition catalogue) Essay by Ramón Vázquez. Caracas: Fundación Palacio de Bellas Artes, 1991.

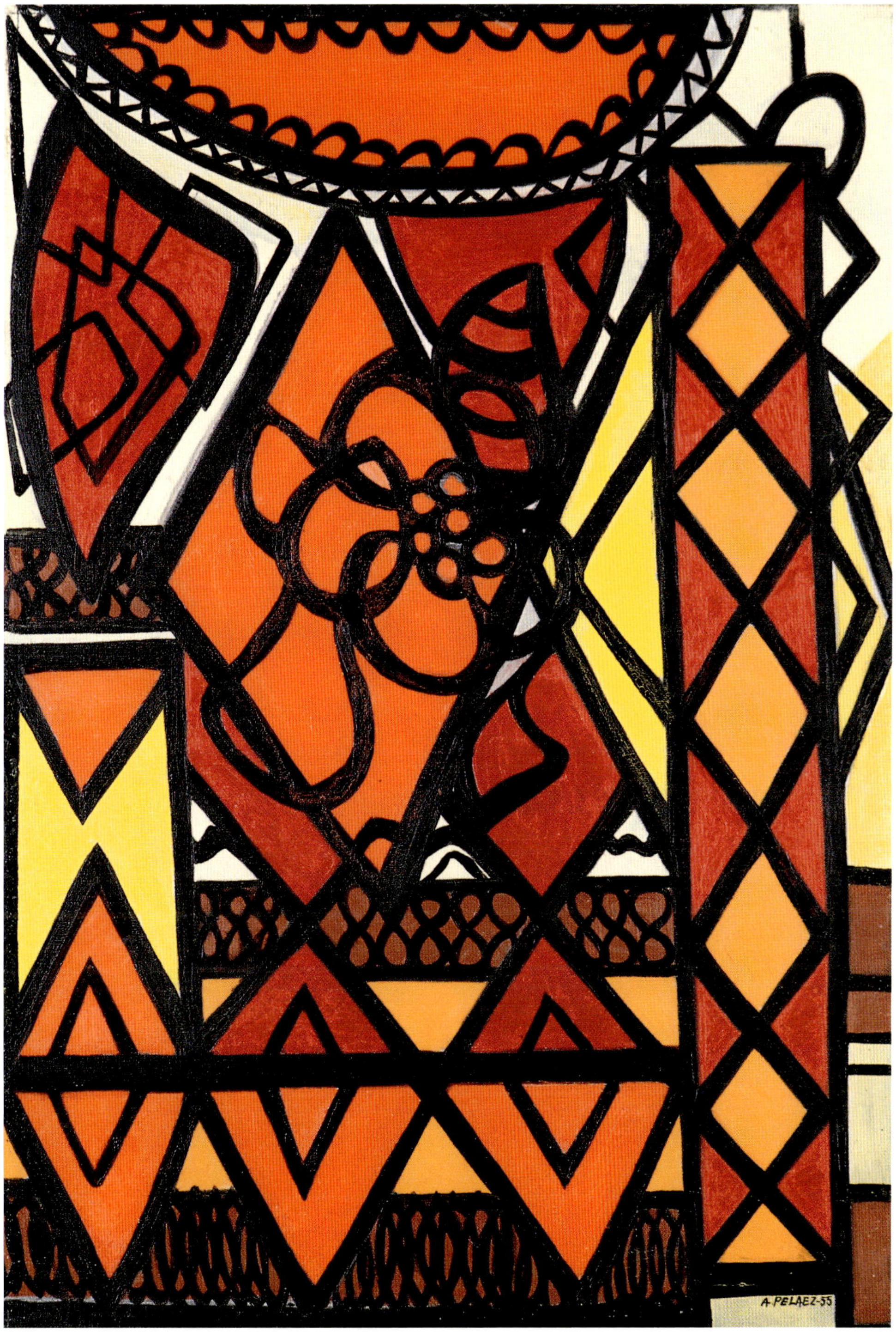

Amelia Peláez

STILL LIFE

1955, Oil on canvas, 35" x 24"

Gift of the Cuban Foundation

Victor Manuel

1897–1969

Manuel García y Valdés was born in Havana in 1897 and died there in 1969. Victor Manuel (his adopted name) graduated from the Academy of San Alejandro and continued his studies informally during two visits to Paris in the 1920s. In Paris he found in the paintings of Jules Pascin and also in those of Paul Gauguin and Paul Cézanne the means to develop his own visual language and primitivist vision of his native land. His one-man show at the Association of Painters and Sculptors in 1927 signaled the beginning of modernist painting in Cuba. After 1927 Victor Manuel kept a presence in the Havana art scene through regular participation in collective and personal exhibitions and as a proselytizer of modern art. In Cuba his paintings are well represented in the National Museum and are also found in numerous private collections. In the United States his paintings are mostly in private collections.

Landscape with Figures is a fine example of Victor Manuel's tropical landscapes, one of his favorite themes. During his long career he painted numerous park, river, and country scenes sparsely populated with adults relaxing and conversing, children playing, and young lovers hugging and kissing. In this painting, done around 1950, his idealized expression of the Cuban countryside as warm, sensual, and timeless reached a high point. The bright palette, highly simplified forms, and sketchy technique visually reinforce the primitivist, rustic subject matter. J.A.M.

Bibliography:
Victor Manuel: Exposición retrospectiva. (Exhibition catalogue) Essay by Jorge Rigol and excerpts of writings by various authors. Havana: Consejo de Cultura, Museo Nacional, 1969.

Victor Manuel: Un innovador en la pintura cubana. (Exhibition catalogue) Essay by Gillermo de Zéndegui. Miami: Museo Cubano de Arte y Cultura, 1982

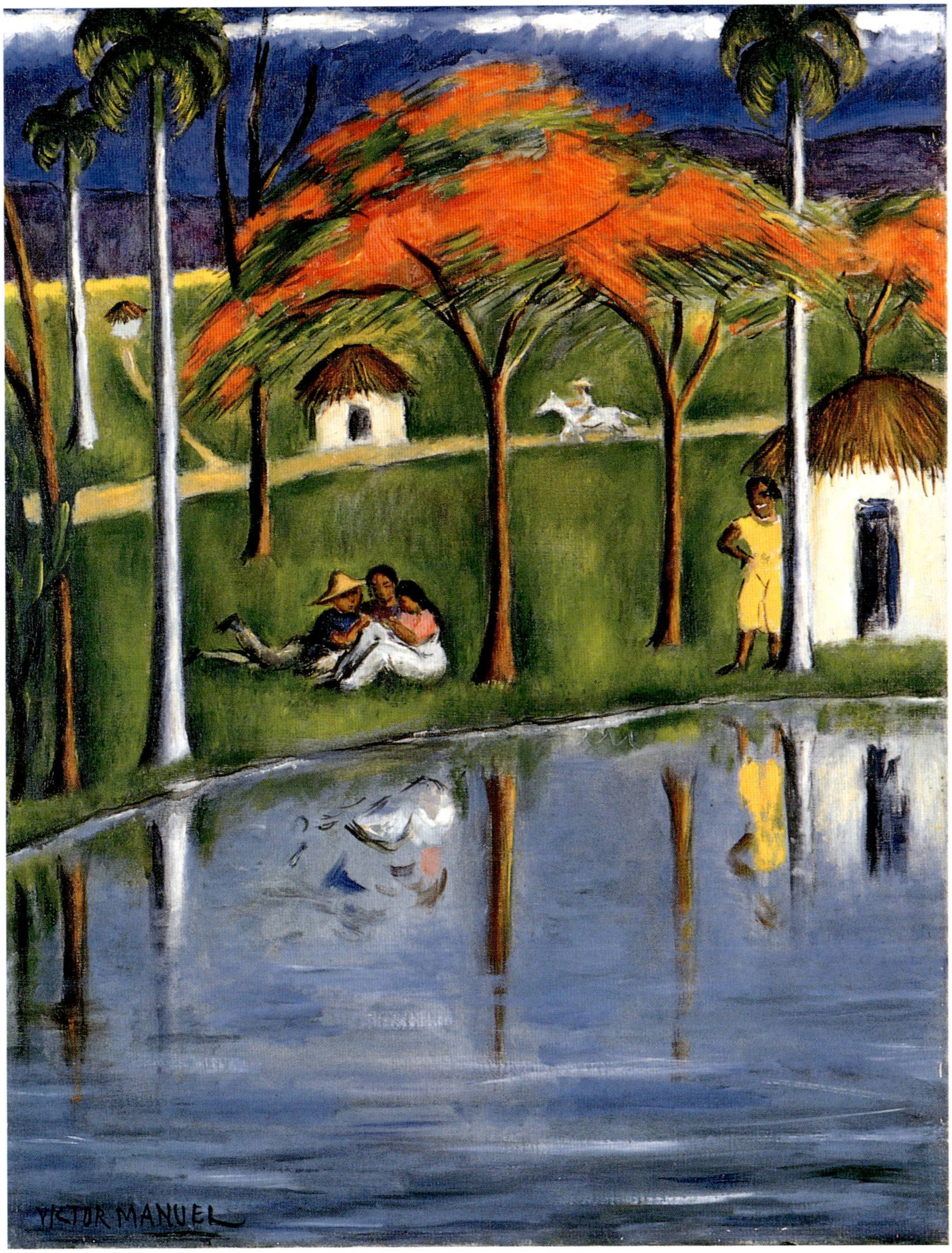

Victor Manuel

Landscape with Figures

Ca. 1950, Oil on canvas, 22" x 17"

Gift of the Cuban Foundation

Carlos Enríquez

1900–1957

Carlos Enríquez Gómez was born in Zulueta, in the province of Las Villas, in 1900 and died in Havana in 1957. His scant artistic education consisted of painting courses in high school, a summer course at the Pennsylvania Academy of Fine Arts in 1924, and personal contact with art and artists in New York (1927–30) and Europe (1930–34), places which he visited for the purpose of expanding his artistic horizons. His reencounter with Cuba in 1934 provided the catalyst for his mature style of transparent color-forms depicting a varied subject matter, which included psychological portraits, erotic nudes, scenes of social protest, and mythical views of the Cuban countryside. He exhibited widely in Cuba and won purchase awards in the National Salons of 1935 and 1938. His paintings are in numerous private and some public collections in the United States, including that of the Museum of Modern Art in New York.

Harlequins, shown in the 1946 Third National Salon of Painting and Sculpture, is a first-rate example of one of Carlos Enríquez's favorite subjects: the female nude. The figure most likely represents his second wife, Eva Frejaville, whom he painted in the nude a number of times. The painting was done about the time that their marriage broke up, which may explain the references to violence and flight. In the 1940s Carlos Enríquez adopted a brighter palette and more vigorous brushmark, moving away from the refined transparencies of his 1930s work toward a bolder, more painterly approach. His nude paintings moved from the expression of sensuality to that of sexuality. This painting shows both of these tendencies in the art of Enríquez at that time. J.A.M.

Bibliography:
Carlos Enríquez, 1900–1957. (Exhibition catalogue) Essay by Gabriela Pogolotti and excerpts of writings by various authors, including the artist. Havana: Museo Nacional, 1979.

Carlos Enríquez. (Exhibition catalogue) Essay by Carlos M. Luis. Miami: Museo Cubano de Arte y Cultura, 1986.

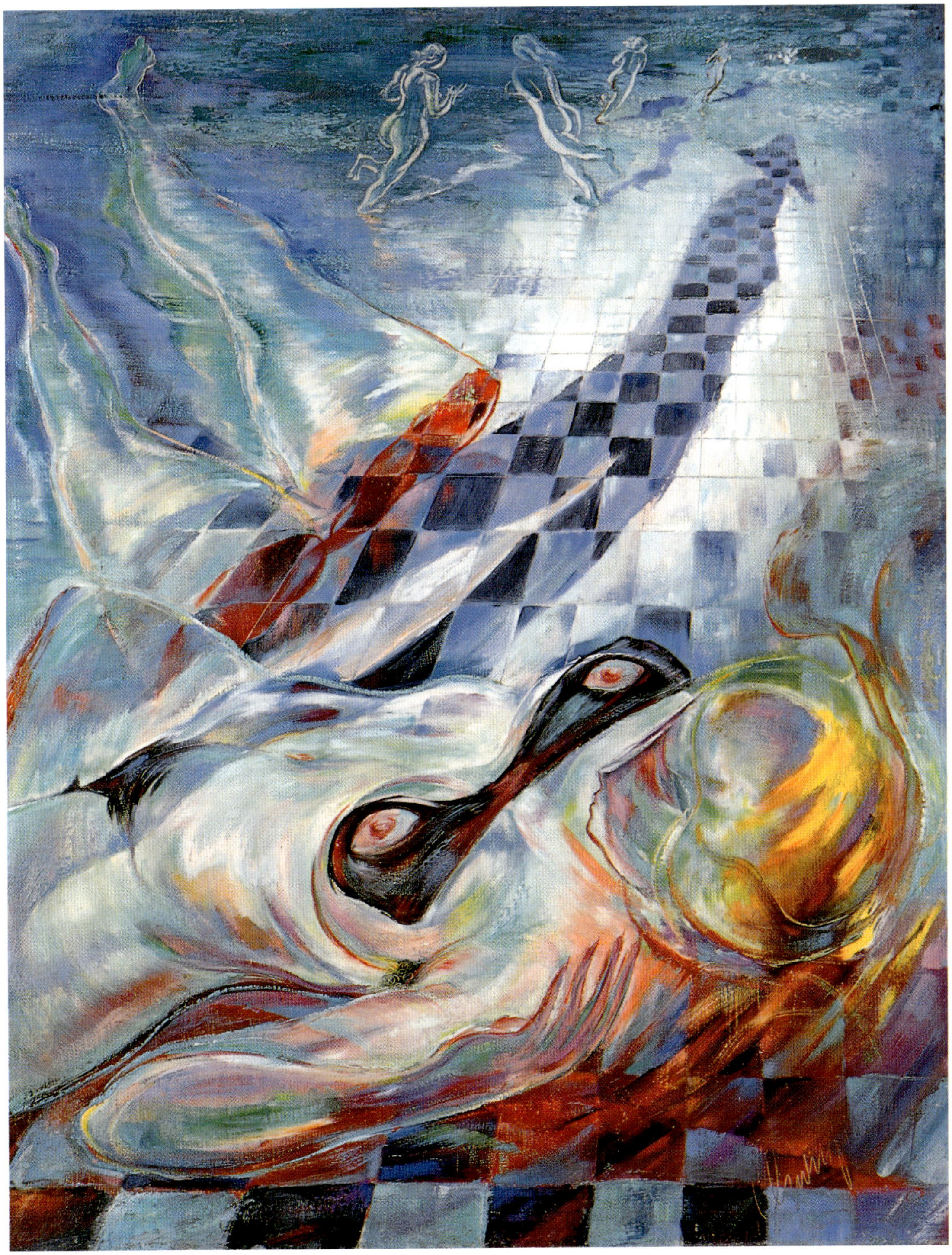

Carlos Enríquez

HARLEQUINS

Ca. 1940, Oil on canvas, 35" x 29"

Gift of the Cuban Foundation

Lorenzo Romero Arciaga

Born 1905

Lorenzo Romero Arciaga still resides in Havana, his birth place. He studied painting and sculpture at the Academy of San Alejandro, abandoning it in the late 1920s for the informal teachings and primitivism of Victor Manuel. He participated in most of the major exhibitions of the 1930s, which helped establish the modernist movement in Cuban art. From 1934 to 1960, he acted as curator and conservator for the Directory of Culture, helping to organize eight national salons of art (1935–59) and taking care of their purchase awards. His paintings are found mostly in private and public collections in Cuba, including that of the National Museum in Havana.

Romero Arciaga's idealized representation of the Cuban peasant's life is seen at its best in *The Cup of Coffee*. In his "naive" style he represents a model peasant family in a scenic interior. The figure of the husband is surrounded by objects and characters suggesting protection, love, beauty, and obligation: a print of Cuba's patron saint, Nuestra Señora de la Caridad, caressing children, a vase of flowers, and the wife bringing coffee. In form and content the painting presents a primitivist vision of life in the Cuban countryside as pleasurable, uncomplicated, and timeless.

J.A.M.

Bibliography:
Juan A. Martínez. *Cuban Art and National Identity: The Vanguardia Painters, 1927–1950*. Gainesville: University Press of Florida, 1994.

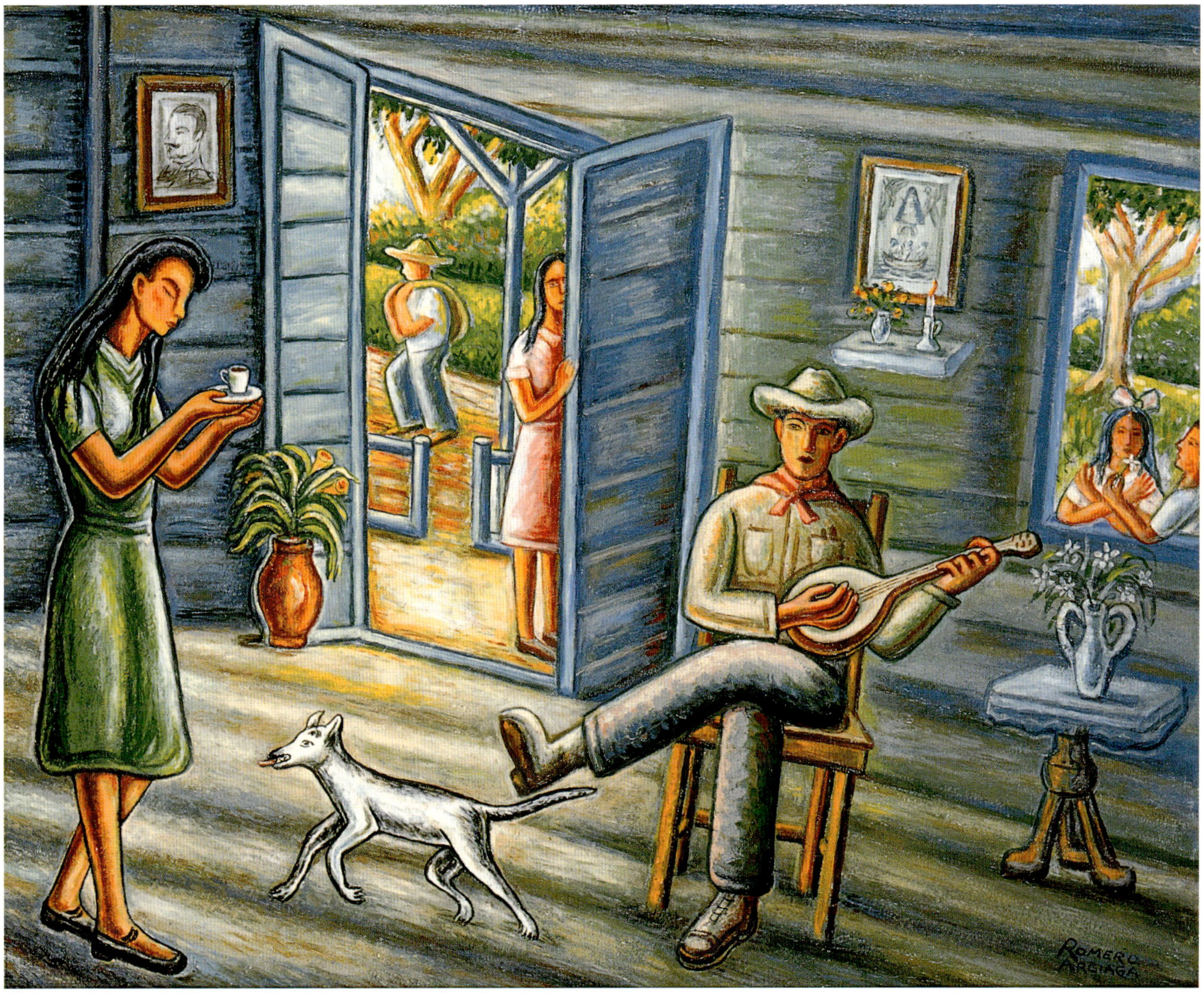

Lorenzo Romero Arciaga

THE CUP OF COFFEE

Ca. 1940, Oil on board, 38" x 48"

Gift of the Cuban Foundation

René Portocarrero

1912–1985

René Portocarrero was born in Havana in 1912 and died there in 1985. He was primarily self-taught, having attended Havana's Academy of San Alejandro only briefly. After a long search, he developed his mature style in the early 1940s, a highly personal figurative expressionism of elaborate forms, strong colors, and a varied subject matter that over time included interiors, festivities, landscapes, religious subjects, still lifes, cityscapes, Afro-Cuban themes, and female figures. In Cuba, Portocarrero exhibited extensively, won numerous awards, and was the subject of three major retrospective exhibitions (1960, 1967, and 1982). He was a prolific artist, and his easel and mural paintings are well represented in Cuban museums, public spaces, and private collections. He also developed an international reputation through personal exhibitions in Latin America, Europe, and the United States. He is represented in the collection of the Museum of Modern Art in New York, that of the Art Museum of the Americas in Washington, D.C., and in numerous private U.S. collections.

Figure in Grey of 1957 is an unusual monochromatic and understated painting. The figure's bold execution is vintage Portocarrero, while the subtle use of color and the dominance of grey counterpoints with his usual rainbow palette. The Cubist-oriented style of the figure suggests not so much the representation of a human being as the construction of a female entity, an approach which runs through most of his paintings of the female figure. His female figures also often evoke a mysterious presence, like in this painting.

J.A.M.

Bibliography:
René Portocarrero, exposición antologica. (Exhibition catalogue) Essays by Antonio Saura, José Lezama Lima, and Alejo Carpentier; poem by Nicolás Guillén. Havana: Museo Nacional, Madrid: Museo Español de Arte Contemporaneo, 1984.

Graciela Pogolotti and Ramón Vázquez, *René Portocarrero*. Havana: Editorial Letras Cubanas, Berlin: Henschel, 1987.

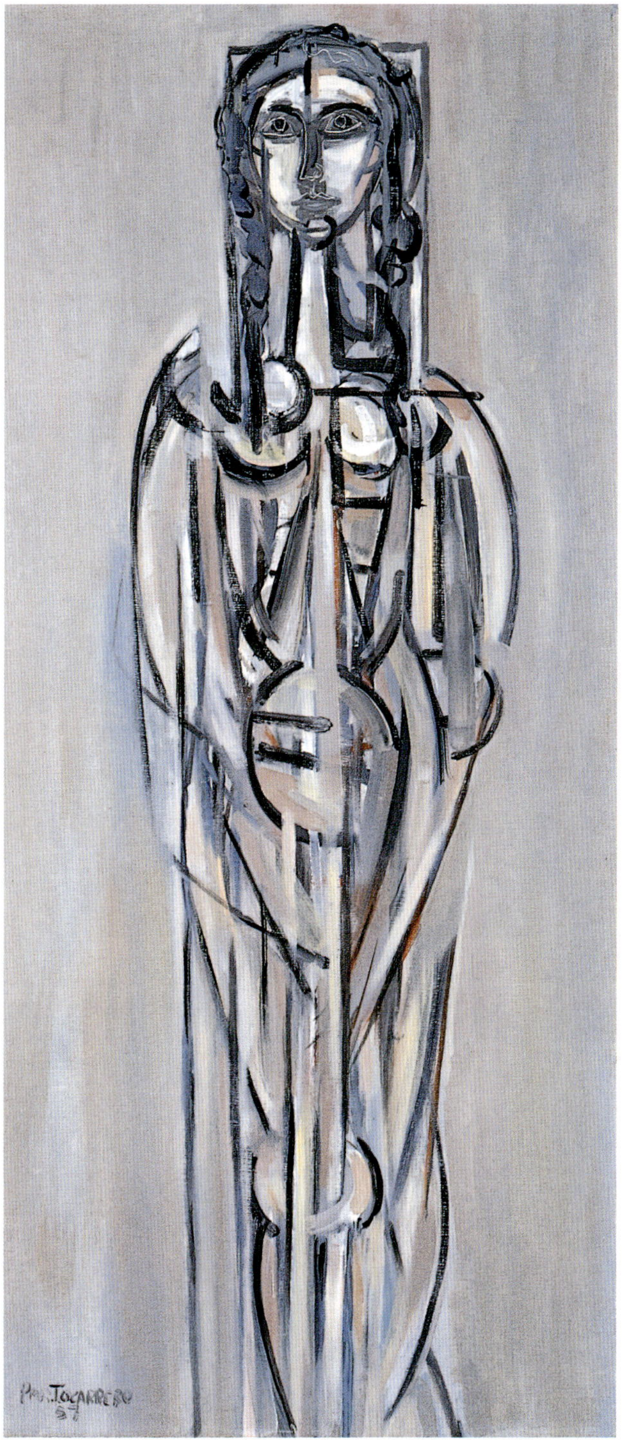

René Portocarrero

FIGURE IN GREY

1957, Oil on canvas, 40" x 18"

Gift of the Cuban Foundation

Mario Carreño

1913–1999

Mario Carreño Morales was born in Havana in 1913. He began his artistic career as an illustrator in the early 1930s in Havana, turning his full attention to painting in 1936 while living in Mexico City and under the inspiration of the Mexican Muralist movement. Later in Paris (1938–39) and in New York (1940), Carreño developed a neo-classical style and subject matter. After his return to Cuba in 1941, he moved toward Expressionism as a more suitable visual language to signify his rediscovered tropical land. Since then Carreño's art has been characterized by technical virtuosity, stylistic change, and poetic imagination. In 1957, he went to live in Santiago de Chile. Carreño has exhibited extensively in Latin America and the United States. His paintings are in the collection of the Museum of Modern Art in New York City, the Art Museum of the Americas in Washington, D.C., and numerous private collections.

Setting Sun of 1955 is a fine example of Carreño's nonfigurative style of that decade. His geometric abstractions stand out for their varied and precise forms, vibrant colors, and dynamic compositions. They also affirm the flatness of the medium through the thin and even application of pigment. Although paintings such as this one emphasize a purely aesthetic experience, its title and some of its forms still point to the world of appearances. J.A.M.

Bibliography:
José Gómez Sicre. *Cuadernos de la Plástica Cubana I-Carreño.* Havana: Ediciones Galería del Prado, 1943

Mario Carreño. *Cronología del Recuerdo.* Santiago de Chile: Editorial Antártica, S.A., 1991.

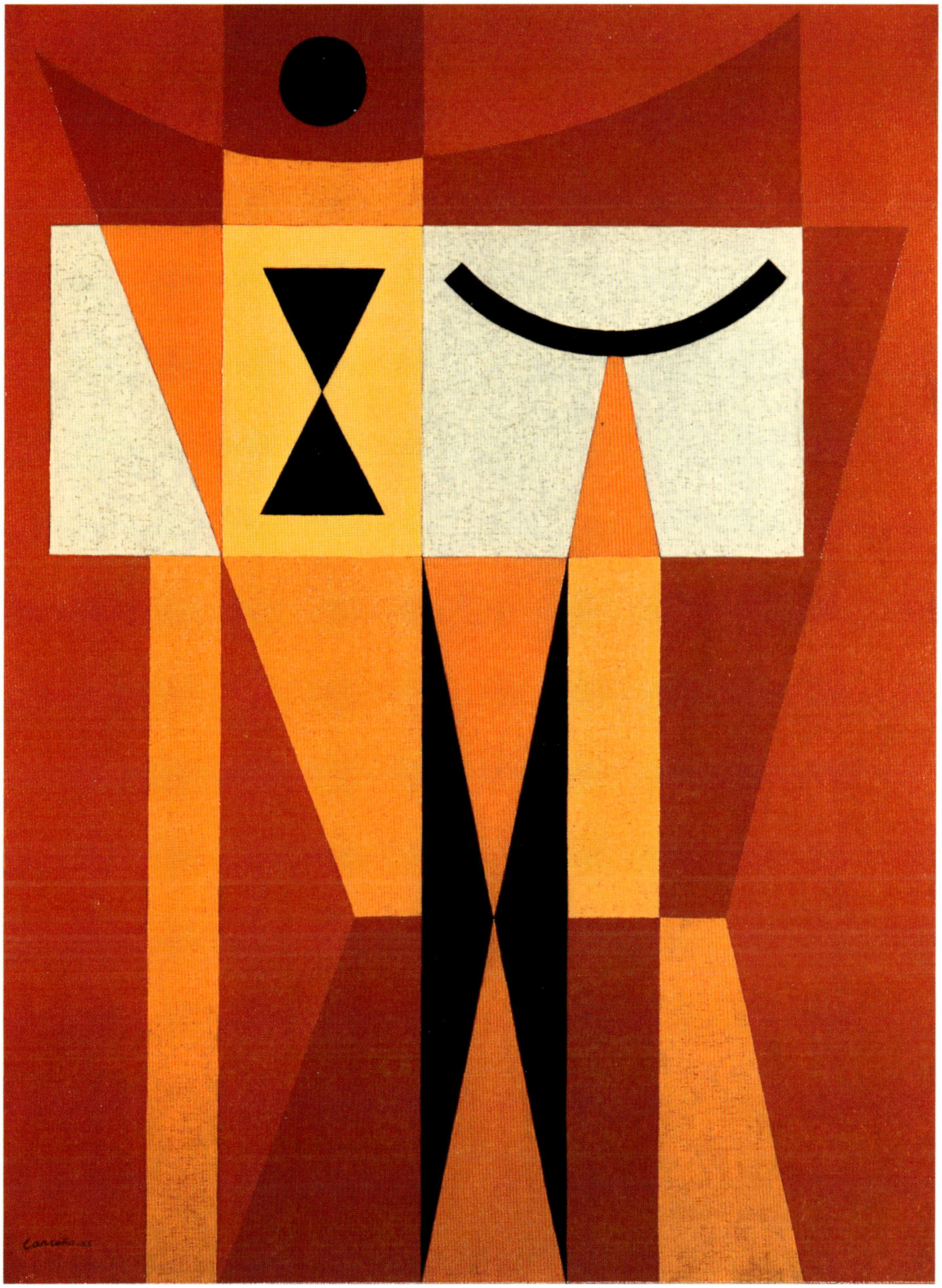

Mario Carreño

Setting Sun

1955, Oil on canvas, 40" x 28"

Gift of the Cuban Foundation

Daniel Serra-Badué

1914–1996

Born in 1914 in Santiago de Cuba, Daniel Serra-Badué received his early art education at age ten at the Escuela Municipal de Bellas Artes of that city. At age thirteen he traveled to New York City to study with Catalán painter José Simont. At fourteen, Serra-Badué was the youngest student ever admitted to the Art Students League in New York. At age fifteen, in 1929, he traveled to Spain to study with Catalán artist Enrique Pascual Monturiol in Barcelona. The following year he returned to Cuba to finish his high school education while he studied with Hernandez Giró. Serra-Badué returned to Spain in 1932, settling in Barcelona. In early 1936, he returned to Cuba for two years, then left for New York where he studied and painted until 1940. Unable to accept a Prix de Rome because of World War II, Serra-Badué studied architecture at the University of Havana. In 1959, the year of the Castro takeover, he was named assistant director of culture for the Ministry of Education in Cuba, but left instead to travel internationally until he became an expatriate in New York in 1962. He died in New Jersey in 1996.

Serra-Badué's first award was a Gold Medal in the 1928 annual drawing competition in New York City. After that first prize at age fourteen, he received hundreds of awards from associations including the American Society of Contemporary Artists, New York; the Bienal Hispano-Americana de Arte, Havana; the National Academy of Design, New York; the Pennsylvania Academy of the Fine Arts; and the Salon Nacional de Cuba, Havana. Serra-Badué was the recipient of two Guggenheim Foundation fellowships and one Cintas Foundation award.

Serra-Badué exhibited widely in the United States, Cuba, Mexico, and Spain, including group exhibitions at the Academia de Bellas Artes, Santiago de Cuba; the Art Institute of Chicago; the Brooklyn Museum; the Carnegie Institute, Pittsburgh; the Museum of Contemporary Hispanic Art, New York; the Museum of Modern Art of Latin America, Washington, D.C.; and the Whitney Museum of American Art, New York.

Serra-Badué's work has been widely collected by museums including the Museo National, Havana; the Germanisches Nationalmuseum, Nuremberg; the Instituto de Cultura Hispánica, Madrid; and the Brooklyn Museum, the Metropolitan Museum of Art, and the Museum of Modern Art, New York.

Serra-Badué's large and impressive *Cuban Sweets* is an important oil from 1957. The painter presents an open box of assorted cookies and candies with pink, white, blue, and gold paper wrappers on a table top in an outdoor patio setting framed by palm fronds and lush green vegetation. The sweets and green table top are slightly tilted toward the viewer in a Braque-like arrangement that accentuates the implied geometry of many of the forms in the composition. Paint is carefully applied with dense bold strokes and modest impasto, which

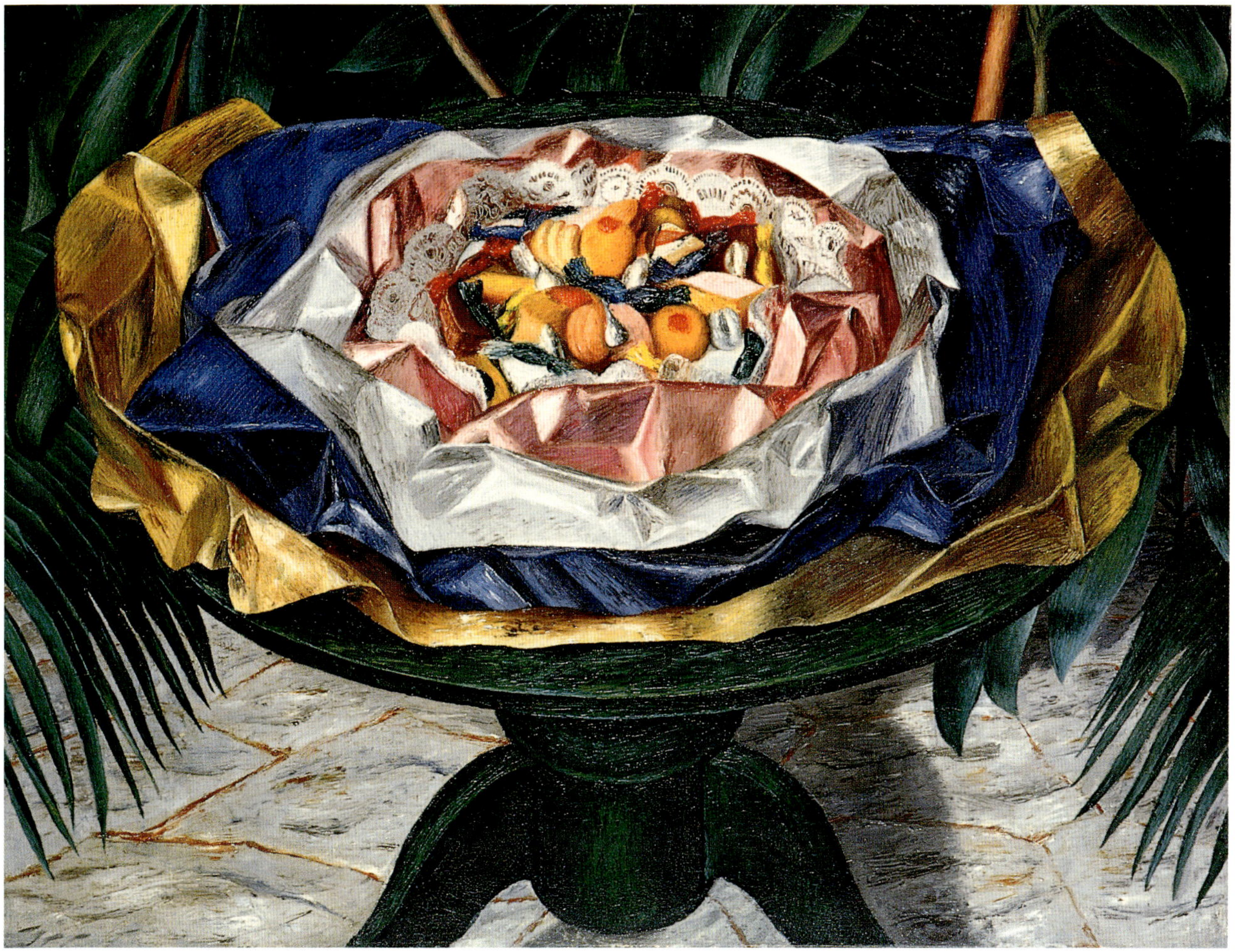

Daniel Serra-Badué

CUBAN SWEETS

1957, Oil on canvas, 29" x 40"

Gift of the Cuban Foundation

highlight the elegant contrast between the sensuality of the sweets and the formal order of the composition. Referring to the traditional box of sweets brought by a suitor, *Cuban Sweets* contains an ambiguous narrative about delicate social relationships in Cuban culture. G.R.L.

Bibliography:

José Gómez Sicre. *Pintura Cubana de Hoy*. Havana, Cuba: Maria Luisa Gómez Mena, 1944.

Dreamt Reality. Marsh Art Gallery, University of Richmond, Virginia, 1994.

Guido Llinás

1923–2005

Guido Llinás was born in 1923 in Pinar del Rio, Cuba. A self-taught painter, he emerged in the early 1950s as a pioneer of nonfigurative art in Cuba. He traveled in the United States and was a leading member of the group Los Once (1953–55), which introduced the abstract expressionism of the New York School to Cuban art. Early on Llinás developed a highly personal version of action painting that he rigorously pursued. In 1963 Llinás moved to Paris, where he was involved in printmaking and painting. He exhibited regularly in Cuba up until 1963 and then exhibited widely in Europe. He was the subject of a retrospective exhibition in San Juan, Puerto Rico, in 1989 and another in Miami in 1997. In the United States his paintings are in numerous private collections.

Composition of 1958 is an excellent example of Llinás's wrist approach to action painting and his dramatic use of black and white. This painting is a precursor to his longest series of paintings, *Pintura Negra* or *Black Paintings* of the 1970s and 1980s, in which deep black paint and strong rhythms inspired by Afro-Cuban music predominated. An integral part of Llinás's signature style was also richly dense textures, affirming the object quality of the painting. J.A.M.

Bibliography:
Llinás, 1989. (Exhibition catalogue) Introductions by Severo Sarduy and Antoine Coron. San Juan: Museo de Arte e Historia, 1989.

Guido Llinás and Los Once from Cuba. (Exhibition catalogue) Essays by Christoph Singler and Juan A. Martínez. Miami: Art Museum of Florida International University, 1997.

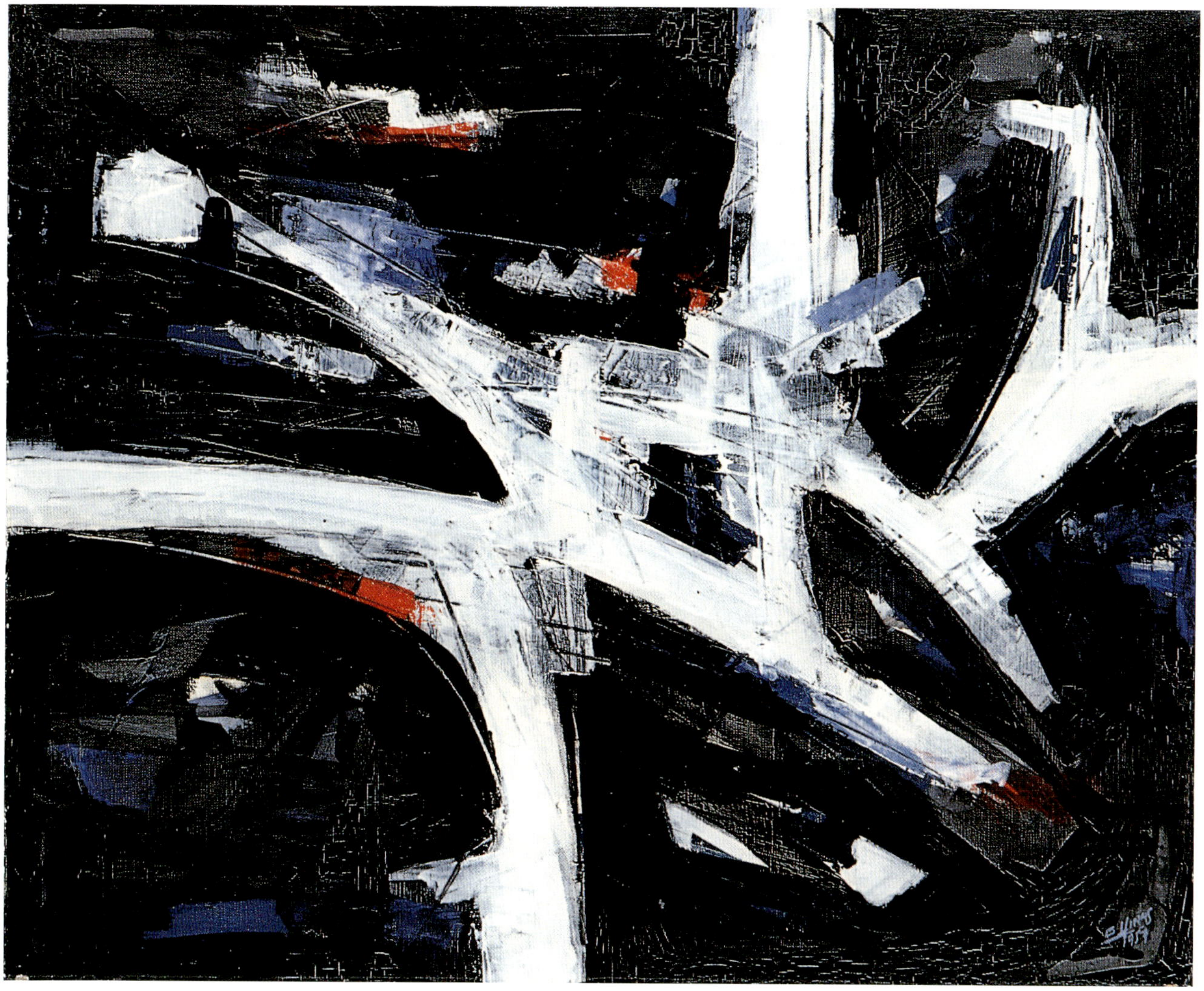

Guido Llinás

Composition

1958, Tempera on canvas, 24" x 28"

Gift of the Cuban Foundation

List of Plates

Listed alphabetically by artist

Latino Paintings
Painting #1,
Late eighteenth century
Oil on canvas, 13" x 10"
p. 48

Painting #2,
Late eighteenth century
Oil on canvas, 13" x 10"
p. 48

Painting #3,
Late eighteenth century
Oil on canvas, 13" x 10"
p. 49

Painting #4,
Late eighteenth century
Oil on canvas, 13" x 10"
p. 49

Guido Llinás
Composition, 1958
Tempera on canvas, 24" x 28"
p. 101

Victor Manuel
Landscape with Figures, ca. 1950
Oil on canvas, 22" x 17"
p. 89

Miguel Melero
Portrait of Aurelio, Son of the Artist, 1906
Oil on canvas, 21" x 25"
p. 57

José A. Bencomo Mena
Keeper of the Roosters, 1934
Oil on canvas, 38" x 29"
p. 81

Armando G. Menocal
Peasant Child, 1936
Oil on board, 19" x 20"
p. 65

Emilio Rivero Merlin
Corner in a Cuban Garden, 1930
Oil on canvas, 30" x 39"
p. 83

Mariano Miguel
La Popa, 1923
Oil on canvas, 41" x 51"
p. 75

Antonio Rodriguez Morey
Symphony in Green, 1899
Oil on canvas, 24" x 36"
p. 67

Sebastian Münster
Map of Novae Insvlae, 1540
Hand-colored wood engraving, 8" x 11"
p. 11

Amelia Peláez
Still Life, 1955
Oil on canvas, 35" x 24"
p. 87

René Portocarrero
Figure in Grey, 1957
Oil on canvas, 40" x 18"
p. 95

Leopoldo Romañach
On the Way to Mass, ca. 1930
Oil on canvas, 59" x 31"
p. 61

Study for a Head, detail, 1926
Oil on canvas, 19" x 17"
p. 62

Italian Peasant,
Early twentieth century
Oil on canvas, 19" x 15"
p. 63

Daniel Serra-Badué
Cuban Sweets, 1957
Oil on canvas, 29" x 40"
p. 99

Esteban Valderrama
The Park of the Brotherhood in Havana, 1957
Oil on canvas, 22" x 18"
p. 85

Photography Credits

Portrait photographs of modern Cuban painters by Berestein, reproduced from *Pintura Cubana de Hoy* by José Gómez Sicre (Havana: Maria Luisa Gómez Meña, 1944).

Photographer unknown, Havana, City Scene, from the collection of Ramiro Fernandez.